Predator-Proof Your Fa

Updated Editi

The

Porn Factor

Pornography &
Child Sexual Abuse

Diane Roblin-Lee

Foreword by
Melodie Bissell

Library and Archives Canada Cataloguing in Publication

Roblin-Lee, Diane, 1945-
   The porn factor : pornography and child sexual
abuse-- the connection / Diane Roblin-Lee.

(Predator-proof your family series ; #5)
Includes bibliographical references.
ISBN 978-1-896213-52-1   E-book ISBN 978-1-896213-64-4

   1. Child sexual abuse. 2. Child pornography.
3. Pornography. I. Title. II. Series: Roblin-Lee, Diane, 1945-
Predator-proof your family series ; #5.

HV6570.R624 2009   362.76   C2009-903697-5
© 2017 Diane Roblin-Lee
First Edition 2009
Second Edition 2017

PUBLISHED IN CANADA
byDesign Media
www.bydesignmedia.ca

COVER DESIGN – Diane Roblin-Lee

Cataloguing data available from Library and Archives Canada

Disclaimer: The opinions expressed in this booklet are those of the author and do not constitute part of the curriculum of any program. The development, preparation and publication of this work has been undertaken with great care. However, the author, publisher, editors, employees and agents of Plan to Protect®, are not responsible for any errors contained herein or for consequences that may ensue from use of materials or information contained in this work. The information contained herein is intended to assist communities, institutions and individuals in establishing effective response to a controversial issue and is distributed with the understanding that it does not constitute legal or medical advice. References to quoted sources are only as current as the date of the publications and do not reflect subsequent changes in law. Where any sourced material may have been inadequately referenced, the author extends a apology. The research has been so extensive that it has been impossible to track every source. Organizations, communities and individuals are strongly encouraged to seek legal counsel as well as counsel from an insurance company when establishing any policy concerned with this topic.

Purpose

The eightfold purpose behind the
Predator-Proof Your Family Series:

- To help families and guardians recognize danger signs in people
  who have access to the children in their care

- To deter people who are fantasizing about molesting
  a child from acting on their fantasies

- To protect children from molestation through raising
  awareness on many levels

- To be aware of the new challenges of parenting in the
  21st century.

- To deepen the understanding of all levels of society affected
  by the molestation of a child

- To find healing for victims and families

- To encourage the kind of justice and community
  action that prevents potential or convicted predators from initial
  offending and re-offending.

- To demonstrate to all those who have been molested that we
  care deeply about what you have endured and, in honour of you,
  are doing all we can to protect other children from sharing your
  experience.

Predator-Proof Your Family Booklet Series
By Diane Roblin-Lee

Booklet #1 – *Why All the Fuss?* ISBN 978-1-896213-48-4
Prevalence, Effects and Trends of Child Sexual Abuse

Booklet #2 – *Who is the Predator?* ISBN 978-1-896213-49-1
Identification – Warning Signs

Booklet #3 – *Predator-Proofing Our Children* ISBN 978-1-896213-50-7
Recognizing the Grooming Process
Parent / Child Education – When the Molester Strikes at Home

Booklet #4 – *Predators in Pews and Pulpits* ISBN 978-1-896213-51-4
The God Factor - Forgiveness?
How Dare They Call Themselves Christians?

Booklet #5 – *The Porn Factor* ISBN 978-1-896213-52-1
Are You Raising a Predator?
The Old Bottom Line - The Buck

Booklet #6 – *It's All About the Brain* ISBN 978-1-896213-53-8
Does Child Molestation Affect Brain Development?
How to Use the Brain in Effective Treatment

Booklet #7 – *When the Worst That Can Happen Has Already Happened*
ISBN 978-1-896213-54-5 Healing for the Victim
Parenting an Abused Child – Coping as the Family of a Predator

Booklet #8 – *Smart Justice* ISBN 978-1-896213-47-7
Community Response to Predators Who Have Served Their Time
Church Response - School Response - Restorative Justice

Booklet #9 – *The Husband I Never Knew* ISBN 978-1-896213-56-9
The true story of Diane Roblin-Lee, ex-wife of a man who, after 38
years of marriage, confessed to being a child molester.

Available online in Paperback and Kindle

Also available through Plan to Protect®
117 Ringwood Dr., Unit #11, Stouffville, ON CAN L4A 8C1
www.plantoprotect.com 1-877-455-3555

Foreword

When our children were young, we had a Christmas party for the neighborhood children. In the loot bags, we gave each child a bookmark for a popular children's website where they could play games, send greeting cards, read funny jokes and solve riddles. A week later, my neighbors questioned why I had sent their children to a porn site. I was horrified. When I dug into the confusion, I discovered that if a child were to miss typing in one small symbol, images of naked men and women would appear, only to be seared on the mind of the child. I was shocked to discover that developers and officers of porn sites deliberately target young minds by addressing or naming pornographic websites similarly to innocent sites, knowing that if they can ensnare children early, they will be able to trap them into porn addiction.

At the 2009 Children's Spirituality Conference in Chicago, Marlene LeFever reported that it takes only three-tenths of a second to frame (establish) a pornographic image in one's mind. This brief view of perverted sexuality will start the wheels of addiction in motion.

Whatever happened to innocence?

I hear of parents who refuse to expose their children to images of the crucifixion, holocaust, and genocide to protect them from the real world – but at the same time place computers in their children's bedrooms, giving them free access to websites that destroy their values, morality, respect and compassion.

When will we stop sitting idly by and say enough is enough? When will we summon our voices and speak boldly on behalf of the innocent? When will we call for stronger legislation regarding the atrocities perpetrated by the purveyors of pornography?

The Internet has become a cesspool of pornography. It has also become a manual used, even by young teens, to learn how to access children for purposes of abuse. Marybeth Elliott, mother of David (*David's Sword*, Tate: 2009), revealed that the teenager who abused her son learned how to do it on the Internet and followed the directions word for word.

Diane Roblin-Lee has said "Enough!" *The Porn Factor* provides a myriad of helpful suggestions on protecting children from those seeking to "groom" them for the purposes of sexual gratification. For those who don't know where to begin, in several of the booklets, Diane provides checklists of suggestions, including how to establish stronger controls on the Internet for limiting criminal access to children.

I recognize this is not fun reading. Many people will avoid reading this Series – either because they can't stomach the contents or because they don't understand how pornography may affect their lives personally.

Ignorance will not erase the reality of the horrors this world has witnessed, nor will it erase the dangers of the Internet. It will not remove the potential risk presented by the family member, the babysitter, the neighbor, the priest, the teacher or the coach who may be grooming your child.

With Diane, I truly hope that this booklet will help you find your voice on behalf of the children.

Melodie Bissell
President, Plan to Protect ®
www.plantoprotect.com

The Porn Factor

The naked human body has always evoked a primal response; whether as a mirror reflection or from eye-to-flesh contact with someone else. But when that vulnerable beauty is exposed to the public as a commodity offered for base consumption in the spirit of degradation, the angels must weep.

If It Bothers You, Why Not Just Ignore It?

And yet those who dare to raise an eyebrow (let alone express concern about the burgeoning porn industry that threatens to assault their children and families) risk being labeled as puritanical, old-fashioned, irrelevant or prudish. They're met with wholesale contempt. "Pornography has always been around," their shrugging critics say. "If you don't like it, leave it alone."

Obviously, no one is going to eliminate pornography. But not to address its harmful effects on people, particularly on children with their sponge-like brains set to absorb all they see and hear, would be like suggesting that we ignore murder, rape or slavery because they've been around since the earliest days.

Thankfully, there were people in the days of deep-south slavery who stood up to the status quo and cared enough about the societal wrongs that they endured ridicule and saw a change.

Pornography is not just a societal wrong. Regardless of the moral stance one may take, the awareness of what it does physically to the brain is sadly lacking. Cavalier users are generally ignorant regarding its actual physical and psychological effects. The ripple effect of what happens to those whose lives surround them is seldom even considered as they click the mouse from porn site to porn site.

Addiction can lock its grip and change the entire course of people's lives even after "light dabbling." Once that grip has locked on, it's no longer a matter of moral choice or deciding whether or not to continue indulging in the offerings of pornography – because choice has been sacrificed to addiction.

When people understand that porn is equally addictive to any drug out there (actually writing new neural pathways in the brain governing the user's sexuality, sexual tastes, and sexual boundaries), they're more likely to tuck their contempt into their back pockets, sit down and be open to conversation.

You think I exaggerate? Read on.

Who am I?

Who am I? I'm someone who had her family shattered and lost everything I held dear as a result of my husband's addiction to pornography and subsequent crimes. My family and his victims have been damaged to the point where our lives and future have been changed forever. Rather than ignore the ability of pornography to do the same thing to other marriages, families, and victims, I'm using my voice to warn unsuspecting people about the consequences of getting trapped in its death grip.

In some sense, this book is a tool of redemption for use against the weapon of pornography that eventually destroyed our family and the victims of my ex-husband. It is a tool that has been forged by the hammer of adversity in our lives. I hope that those who read it will short-circuit the effects of pornography by not indulging in it – or, if already watching it, will commit to a program of restoration, such as some suggested here, and regain access to a healthy life.

People wonder how I could have lived in a marriage where there was so much deception that my husband was a virtual stranger. The answer is that deception hides truth and when one trusts someone, there is no feeling of needing to look for signs of wrong-doing. It is only when one understands the signs of deception that one is stirred to search for them. I hope that the research contained herein will move readers to greater awareness of realities.

Trying to put the lessons I've learned to work for others has not been an easy journey, but the road to healing is an important one to take, particularly if others can be helped along the way. Pornography and its fruit need to be exposed for the critical dangers they present.

Virtual Crack Cocaine

Internet pornography has been called "the new crack cocaine."[1] The similarities between pornography and drug use are undeniable. Watching porn becomes a habit that escalates into an obsession and can often evolve far beyond anything the user ever planned or anticipated.

As some consumers develop tolerance, the porn that once excited them begins to seem boring. So, they may try to compensate by spending more time with it or seeking out more hard core material to regain the excitement. Soon, themes of aggression, violence, and increasingly "edgy" acts may start to creep into their habits and fantasies, creating new neural pathways.

Continued use drives the need for stronger, more perverted images. What begins as viewing a picture has the potential to grow not only

1. Dr. James Dobson

into an addiction, but into an encounter with a victim. Of course, not all porn users become child molesters and lose their homes and families; but of those that do, none imagined that to be a possibility when they first began viewing pornography.

While many assume that, in order to develop an addiction, an addictive substance is required, specialists know that's incorrect; it is the brain response, the dopamine rush, that is the key to the individual wanting it again and again, in increasing quantities.

Like a drug being released into the system, the watching of pornography results in the brain releasing endorphins, creating an intense feeling of euphoria and a hunger for subsequent use. The "high" makes repeated viewing much more tempting...and highly likely.

Like any addictive substance, porn triggers the release of dopamine into the reward center of the brain. The reward center's function is to make a person feel good whenever he or she does something healthy; like eating a great meal, making love, or returning from an invigorating walk. Known as a "high," it makes the person want to repeat the behavior again and again.

Constant viewing of pornography physically alters the brain. Deterioration can happen after just a few views.

As many know, the pre-frontal cortex controls the activity of the rest of the brain. It's basically what makes us human. If it is damaged, the ability to make good decisions will be compromised. People will act more impulsively. Where a normal brain will have good blood flow, affording the person the ability to make reasoned choices, a sex-addicted person will have poor blood flow to the pre-frontal cortex; the result being loss of ability to control the brain properly or make good decisions. The brain will look bumpy instead of smooth and it will be increasingly full of holes. The research conducted by scientists featured in the "Conquer Series"[2] is fascinating, showing photos of normal brains compared with those of cocaine addicts and pornography addicts.

For someone who has regularly been feeding on Internet pornography, his or her brain will be so riddled with holes that the ability to just stop using porn will be an impossibility, no matter how much he or she tries. Addiction means loss of control. It means being enslaved. It means having lost the ability to make a choice whether or not to watch it.

Having lost the ability to choose, or make good choices, however, doesn't mean that an addicted person is not responsible for his or her actions. The responsibility comes with having become addicted in the first place. Thus one is accountable for any bad decisions or criminal activities that may have transpired in a state of porn addiction.

The good news is that the fantastic neuro-plasticity of the brain makes it amazingly flexible and capable of restoration. With a structured approach and accountability, someone who genuinely wants freedom from addiction can have his or her mind renewed or restored. It may take two or three years of detox and rebuilding to have any chance of being back in control, but the potential for healing is there. Restoring the relationships lost in the process, however, may not be so easy. The best cure is always not getting addicted in the first place.

Unlike drugs, pornography is available around the clock with no cost beyond an Internet hookup and a computer. In an article for *PsychReg*, psychologist Dr. Julie Newberry writes: "My therapeutic experience is that a person who views child abuse images, though committing a sexual offense, is not necessarily a pedophile. A

---

2. See page 72.

pedophile has a primary sexual interest in children. I suggest that for some people, it is porn addiction rather than pedophilia, which is the cause. A person, usually a man, who has no sexual interest in children, can find himself 'crossing the line.'"

She continues to describe her experience, saying, "(My clients) didn't go onto the Internet with the intention of looking at child abuse images, but ended up there. They couldn't understand why they continued to do something that disgusted them and which they knew was illegal. I suggest that each of them became desensitized to mild porn and sensitized to extreme porn. Their higher thinking brain, compromised by addiction, could not win the battle, even when it came to viewing child abuse images. Porn sex was too powerful a need and withdrawal too difficult."

The front-line battle against pornography is in the brain. While the purveyors, producers, and marketers may put the raw material out there, the front line of the fight is in the brain of the user. It is there that one successfully resists the onslaught – or suffers destruction as a result of engagement.

While not every porn consumer will end up turning to illegal content, many do. Porn is anything but harmless. In too many cases, the consumer ends up becoming consumed.

From Cave Dweller to 21st Century "Porn Connoisseur"

It's true – sexually explicit material has been around since cave dwellers experimented with drawings on their walls. In the 1860's, the ancient city of Pompeii was excavated. In the process, a lot of sexually explicit paintings and pottery were discovered – not just innocuous drawings of people and animals, but explicit drawings of bestiality, orgies and phallic decorations.

12

People have been thinking about weird ways to indulge their sexual urges and using various methods of depicting their activities since the invention of the stylus. However, those who contend that pornography is harmless and normal, just because it has been around for centuries, probably haven't thought about the fact that the history of pornography, as we know it, is relatively recent.

Pornographic films are only as old as filmography itself. Watching actors on a screen interact sexually has a far different effect on the brain than just flipping through pages of static images. Erotic novels didn't hit the bookshelves until 1748.

Hugh Hefner first donned his pajamas and gave birth to *Playboy* magazine in 1953, following his impregnation with the revolutionary philosophy of the 1948 and 1953 Kinsey Reports.

Another thing that has changed, is the degree of perversion involved in the production of pornography. The producers know that addiction creates an insatiable appetite for more and so they have to keep coming up with new material.

The problem is that they can't get any more raw material with which to work. Humans aren't growing any more parts to feed the fascination. Women still just have two breasts and a vagina. Men haven't sprouted anything besides penises. Three parts for women – one part for men. Period. That's all the purveyors of pornography have to use. So they have to get creative.

In order to change it up and maintain business momentum, the gazillion-dollar porn industry has had to pervert sexuality and normal bodily functions. (I apologize for the graphic nature of this paragraph and suggest that particularly sensitive readers skip the rest of it. I include this material only because it demonstrates a degree of the deterioration of our society.) So – they introduced oral, anal and genital sex between women and dogs, horses, pigs and all kinds of animals. Then came the bathroom games, including golden showers (urination), eating feces and painting them all over faces and bodies. Mutilation was sexualized with fish hooks through genitalia, fists in rectums and mousetraps on breasts. Champagne glasses were filled with ejaculate. Orgies featured oral and anal sex in groups. Torture and even murder were sexualized.[3]

Besides the degree of perversity, what has changed is that people who liked to spend their time looking at drawings, photos or videos of other people's parts used to have to go looking for them. Suddenly, it's as though a tidal wave of smut[4] has washed over society, showing up in practically every advertisement, television program, movie and Internet porn mill. Sex sells in a society where people are preoccupied with looking at other people's parts.

We are becoming so accustomed to seeing images of naked and near-naked people that it's no longer an oddity. People are doing the 'full monty' on prime-time television. The first time I saw people having actual intercourse as I surfed through the channels, I was stunned! Why would I – or anyone else – want to watch that? And then came the "Naked News," where so-called news anchors systematically stripped, to the point of being completely naked, throughout the process of delivering a news story. Can someone please explain to me why we need the context of nudity to understand world events?

But the worst – the worst evidence of the degradation of pornography has been the sexualization of children for the consumption of individuals too sick to care about their own descent into Hades.

---

3. Minnery, Tom (1986). Pornography; A Human Tragedy, Wheaton, Illinois, Tyndale House Publishers Inc., Dr. J. Dobson, p. 35.
4. In modern times, the word, "smut" is most often heard to reference pornography. It is derived from a German word meaning, "dirt." It has nothing to do with the erotic sexuality of a healthy marriage and is generally recognized as exceeding its boundaries.

Porn – or Erotica?

Defenders of pornography like to feign artistic importance, citing appreciation for erotic poetry and sculptures...but can erotic poetry really be fairly compared to today's endless stream of free, violent hard core porn? Really? C'mon – a comparison of apples to apples can't substitute kiwi fruit and pretend they're the same thing.

The defenders quibble over the meaning of the word "pornography." The thing is that where erotica generally refers to sexual relations between consenting adults, pornography involves more than that. It refers to explicit or implied depictions of impersonal sexual activity where a child or an adult is objectified and portrayed as a one-dimensional, dehumanized object for sexual use or displays of the power of one individual over another.

The "Pornographication[5]" of Society

My new word. "Pornographication" is a good word. No other word adequately describes what is happening. We are changing from a culture characterized by moral integrity and character to one so suffused by pornography that it has become part of our fiber.

For those of us who do not choose to immerse our children and grandchildren in cultural trash, the task of raising them to be people of integrity and moral fiber has become daunting indeed: exhausting – discouraging – sometimes futile.

In today's media environment, children put in an average of 40 hours per week consuming its offerings. Just when parents think they've solved the problem by installing the latest filters, they get in the car

---

5. Pornographication – "the conversion of an individual, group or society from acceptance of societal standards, modesty and decency to acceptance of writings, pictures, films and behavior (generally considered obscene) intended primarily to arouse perverted sexual desire." (D.R-L).

for a pleasant family outing, only to subject the children all along the highway to steamy Ralph Lauren and Victoria Secret billboards.

Just as non-smokers are forced to breathe the second-hand smoke of those who insist on using tobacco, those who do not choose to look at sexually explicit material are now sensually assaulted by second-hand smut at every turn. No one can live in North America in the 21st century without absorbing it. So much for democracy and the freedom of choice.

The age-appropriate sectors of the media marketplace are supposedly segregated to protect children from seeing material that would interfere with their healthy development. However, entertainment ratings have become all but meaningless. All streams of media, even good ole' comic books, have become highly sexualized.

Today's PG-13 ratings equate to the "R" ratings of the early 1990's. For instance, the 1994 movie "The Santa Clause" was rated PG, while its sequel, with an equivalent amount of profanity, sexual references, and violence, was rated "G.[6]"

All sectors of entertainment compete with all other sectors because there is only so much time that people can give to entertainment. Thus, as cable television increases its sleaze factor, broadcast television does the same thing, dragging prime-time television into the realm of adult entertainment.

When lines of tiny tot clothing are designed with adult sensuality in mind, it's time for a wake-up call. Manipulation of the morality barometer has a direct bearing on the rise in child abuse incidents. By closing our eyes to the downward slide, we are contributing, not only to the pornographication of society but to the sexual abuse of children.

---

6. Reavill, Gil (2005). SMUT; A SEX INDUSTRY INSIDER (AND CONCERNED FATHER) SAYS ENOUGH IS ENOUGH, London, England, Penguin Books, Ltd., p. 137.

A Harmless Pacifier?

The ordinary joe, who regularly picks up a couple of "skin magazines" at the newsstand, loves to point out that it's better for men to look at pornography than to actually molest a child or act out some other kind of perversion.

Wrong, says Julian Sher, author of *One Child at a Time*. "Looking doesn't deter doing; study after study shows that 35 to 40 percent of those arrested for pornography possession are hands-on abusers."[7]

In order for there to be child pornography, someone has to be molested, and so the very act of indulging in the fantasies it evokes contributes to its manufacture.

Increased exposure to the images leads to addiction, increasing the desire of child porn addicts for increasingly stimulating images. After feeding themselves with more and more graphic pictures, the point comes where pictures aren't enough and they want real interaction with a child. The evidence that there is a direct correlation between watching child pornography and eventually indulging in the sexual abuse of children is overwhelming.

Pornography desensitizes people to the pain suffered by the victims and glorifies the apparent pleasure of the assailant.

Deviant activity is often falsely linked with pleasurable sexual responses, increasing the confusion factor in viewers. When viewers watch children being abused sexually over and over again, their inhibitions gradually break down, and they want to imitate what they have learned. They begin to think that because they're frequently witnessing this kind of behavior, it's widespread and more acceptable than they previously thought.

---

7. Sher, Julian (2007). *One Child at a Time,* Random House Canada.

When they feed on images of perversion, regular sex becomes boring and unsatisfying. They hunger for something more, something less attainable, something with a titillating element of danger.

The Internet – Trojan Horse of the 21st Century

In the *Aeneid*, the poet Virgil tells of the fall of Troy in the 1100's. Having been unsuccessful in their efforts against Troy, the Greeks built a huge wooden horse and left it outside the walls of Troy. They then pretended to sail away, defeated, in their ships. After a duplicitous Greek prisoner convinced them that the horse was sacred and would bring the protection of the gods, the Trojans decided to pull the giant wooden horse into their city. Little did they know that Odysseus and other warriors were hidden in its body. That night, as Troy slept, the Greeks crept out of the belly of the horse and opened the city gates for the rest of the warriors who had returned from a nearby island.

While the Internet has revolutionized society in remarkable ways, the enemies in its underbelly have invaded our homes from within. It has become a unique enabler of child-porn offenders. The more technically astute they become, the more images become available to them.

By creating new ways of offending, the Internet has spawned destructive addictions and criminal obsessions.

MindGeek is a Pandora's box in the realm of Internet pornography. A private company headquartered in Luxembourg, with offices in Dublin, Hamburg, London, Los Angeles, Houston, Miami, Montreal, and Nicosia, it owns and operates the most popular hard core porn websites around today. Over the years, this gigantic enterprise has carefully comprised its many domains in order to offer easily accessible pornography to its viewers. Though you'd never guess by reading their glitzy promotional materials or seemingly mainstream careers page, it now owns a majority of the best-known names in mainstream pornography: Pornhub, Brazzers, Webcams.com, Xtube, Redtube, YouPorn, some of Playboy's assets, and dozens more.

Online MBA compiled some 2010 stats (the latest I could find) re Internet pornography:

1. Twelve percent of the websites on the Internet are pornographic – that's 24,644,172 sites.

2. Every second, $3,075.64 is being spent on pornography and 28,258 users are viewing porn.

3. Forty million Americans are regular visitors to porn sites. One in three porn viewers is female.[8] 70 percent of men, aged 18-24 visit porn sites in a typical month.

4. In the USA, Internet porn pulls in $2.84 billion per year. The entire worldwide industry pulls in $4.9 billion yearly.

5. Two point five billion e-mails per day are pornographic – that's eight percent of all e-mails.

6. Twenty-five percent of all search engine requests are pornography related. That's 68 million per day.

7. Thirty-five percent of all internet downloads are pornographic.

8. The top pornographic search terms are: "sex," "adult dating," and "porn."

9. Utah has the nation's highest online porn subscription rate per thousand home broadband users: 5.47.

---

8. It's possible that some of these are men posing as women.

10. Thirty-four percent of internet users have experienced unwanted exposure to porn, either through pop-up ads, misdirected links or e-mails.

11. There are 116,000 searches for "child pornography" every day.

12. The average age at which a child first sees porn online is 11.

13. Twenty percent of men admit to watching porn online at work. Thirteen percent of women do. The average porn site visit lasts six minutes and 29 seconds.

14. The least popular day for viewing porn is Thanksgiving Day. The most popular day of the week for viewing porn is Sunday.

Notable Entrepreneurs - Change Agents of Morality

Pornography is defined as, *"Books, photographs, magazines, art, or music designed to excite sexual impulses and considered by public authorities or public opinion as in violation of accepted standards of sexual morality.9"*

In trying to figure out how we got here, how pornography went mainstream, we have to follow both the money trail and the trail of the popularization of material that is *"considered by public authorities or public opinion as being in violation of accepted standards of sexual morality."*

The porn industry generated over 13 billion in sales in 2006 and is growing like a forest afire. According to Adult Video News, an estimated 11,000 hard-core porn movies are produced in the United States annually. According to ABC News, while a hit movie can bring in as much as $1 million — adult movies have a very long

9. The American Heritage® New Dictionary of Cultural Literacy, Third Edition, Copyright © 2005 by Houghton Mifflin Company.

shelf life and can keep selling for years after their initial release Most performers see little of the profits. They get only a flat fee, varying from $350 to $1,000 for a conventional sex scene to a few thousand dollars for more extreme sex. That, in itself, is abusive.

Two already-mentioned figures arise in any discussion of the roots of the "sexual revolution." These are Alfred Kinsey and Hugh Hefner.

Alfred Kinsey was the first major figure to step out of societal norms and emerge as a catalyst for change. By cloaking his personal predisposition for pedophilia in academia, he justified his activities and "research" as the science of "sexology." In 1947, he founded the Institution for Sex Research at Indiana University and, in 1948, published *Sexual Behavior in the Human Man* which was followed in 1953 by *Sexual Behavior in the Human Female*. These became known as the "Kinsey Reports," two books that claimed to explain human sexual behavior through conducting research on masturbation, premarital sex, and adultery.

The books were not only shocking to the culture of the day but widely criticized for the methods used to collect the data. The claims made in the reports came not only from personal interviews but from Kinsey's personal observation and involvement with his coworkers in sexual activity. There were even reports of him provoking and observing the molestation of young children for the sake of "research."

Nevertheless, the Kinsey Reports sold three-million copies, gave birth to the "sexual revolution" and amassed a fortune for the author.

Hugh Hefner, "the Hef," saw a chance to make money from the changing cultural views, so he ran with the Kinsey claims and devoted his life to imposing the "new sexuality." Prior to this, conversations about sexuality, politics, and women's rights had not been welcomely regarded in the public square. With the publishing of the "adult entertainment" magazine *Playboy*, Heffner became an iconic figure in the acceptance of pornography as we know it today. To maximize sales of his new magazine, he had to change porn's image from creepy to sophisticated and mainstream, so he put pornographic photos next to essays and articles written by respected authors. The magazines were grabbed from the shelves. The first edition sold over 50,000 copies, and *Playboy* became a multimillion-dollar enterprise. The face of porn was lifted to look like nothing more than harmless pleasure engaged in by successful individuals.

Hefner was notoriously quoted as saying, *"The notion that Playboy turns women into sex objects is ridiculous. Women are sex objects. If women weren't sex objects, there wouldn't be another generation. It's the attraction between the sexes that makes the world go 'round. That's why women wear lipstick and short skirts."* Nevertheless, following the feminist revolution, it became trendy for females to claim an interest in pornography and all things male. Go figure.

To say *Playboy* changed our society's perspective on pornography is an understatement. Suddenly, adult-only images were readily available and the Playboy Mansion and reality show, "The Girls Next Door" made a life of pornography, objectification, and casual sex seem glamorous and desirable. How many people struggling with an all-consuming porn obsession would say that their first accidental exposure to sexually explicit material as a child came with flipping through one of their dad's "magazines?" And, oh ya, the money trail? Hefner amassed an estimated $43 million fortune off the strapless backs of the women he objectified.

These cultural change-agents were more than successful in their entrepreneurial / self-justifying / revolutionizing efforts. The television and film industry took up the baton of change with the release of *Blue Movie* (1969), directed by Andy Warhol. Then came *Mona*

(1970), and *Deep Throat* (1972). Thinking themselves smart, thousands of people popped the infamous Linda Lovelace tape cassette into their new video players and sat around to watch. The producer of *Deep Throat*, the Lovelace movie, invested $25,000.00 and earned more than $50 million in profits.[10]

Videocassette recorders, phone sex services, home computers and pay television replaced the hard-to-duplicate 8-mm film, still photos and magazines delivered in brown paper wrappers – with live action in full technicolor. Millions of calls were made to dial-a-porn services. With video came the new boom years for pornography. Suddenly, the "Golden Age" of porn was upon us.

As pornography began its overthrow of innocence, the world was awash in flower power and any voices that warned against the new moral liberties were not welcome. The 1970 Presidential Commission on Obscenity and Pornography concluded that pornography was harmless and that it even had potential therapeutic value.[11] When the social scientists, on whose work this conclusion was based, told the world that porn was harmless, the floodgates opened and pornography quickly became increasingly explicit, degrading and violent.

But again questioning the schizophrenic nature of the playboy philosophy, why, in October of 2017, was Harvey Weinstein arrested for simply livin' the Hefner-styled life if Hefner was supposed to be such a brilliant catalyst for change?[12]

10. Minnery, Tom (1986). Pornography: A Human Tragedy, Wheaton, Illinois: Tyndale House Publishers p.53.
11. Minnery, Tom (1986). Pornography: A Human Tragedy, Wheaton, Illinois: Tyndale House Publishers p.115.
12. Harvey Weinstein is an American film producer and former film executive, co-founder of Miramax. Following numerous allegations of sexual harassment, sexual assault, and rape against him, Weinstein was fired by his company's board of directors and expelled from the Academy of Motion Picture Arts and Sciences.

Women and Pornography

While the feminist revolution gave a no-brainer boost to equal pay and opportunity movements, it had its downsides. Instead of standing their ground as authentic women with honest attitudes and values, many thought they had to deny their femininity and embrace traditional male attributes. They sold out and diminished our gender. They tried to become the gender they were fighting. Shock value was everything. What could be more shocking than to have a woman claim to enjoy watching others of their gender dehumanized, humiliated or perhaps portrayed as some robotic, sexual gladiator?

The 1960's and 70's were confusing years for women. In 1976, researcher Shere Hite published her revolutionary treatise on female sexuality, denying that there were major differences in arousal rates between men and women. *The Hite Report* became a rallying cry for feminists and an international best-seller. But Hite's results were, if anything, less scientific than Kinsey's. Highly publicized surveys in the 1970s from *Redbook*, *Playboy*, and others had similar problems. Amid all the hoopla, the world of interest in pornography was extended to include women.

While the number of female child sexual abusers is markedly lower than male abusers, researchers have documented evidence that women who expose themselves to pornography are just as likely as men to trivialize rape and to assume that a rape victim was probably promiscuous and wanted rough sex. For a mind tuned to pornography, everything develops sexual overtones, and so, when a child is abused, it's not such a big deal. The sexualization of a child becomes just part of the smutty mosaic of life.

Who are these females who have bought into the acceptability of pornography? And what is there in the female psyche that would allow, or even welcome, degradation of their gender?

The book *Fifty Shades of Grey,* a purported "love story" that involved so-called kinky sex, particularly sadomasochism, sold over 100 million copies. The movie grossed $571,006,128. The story line centers around the relationship between a young college virgin, Ana, and a wealthy billionaire, Christian Grey, who 'romances' Ana into his world of BDSM (bondage, dominance, submission, and sadomasochism). He gets her to sign a mutual business contract that requires her to engage in acts of BDSM with him in return for living the 'dream' with a good-looking guy in a super-rich lifestyle. "The dramatic array of BDSM implements in Christian's bedroom to secure Ana during floggings, slapping, strangulation, etc., is enough to rival a medieval torture chamber.[13]"

So what is there about women that could make a young virgin even consider signing such a covenant – and what is there about our culture that would make people so fascinated by such a story-line that they would spend over $500,000,000.00 to see the movie? What has happened to the minds of female movie-watchers – who knew what the movie would be about – that would cause them to think it's okay to watch a young girl being tortured?

Part of it is the old problem that many vulnerable women are willing to sell themselves out because they don't really know who they are and don't have the confidence to assert themselves. They think that if the media is telling them a particular movie is going to be cool, and that if their friends seem to think it's going to be cool, they need to participate and see it.

The porn industry is well down the road to defining our sexuality. Whatever perversions they use to push the envelope becomes the new cultural fad. Many women are afraid of being seen as 'out of

13. Huffpost, The Blog by Dr. Ludy Green, 03/04/2015

step' with today's society. Who wants to be called a "prude?"

But sadomasochism? How can a woman find it enjoyable – or enjoy watching it? According to an article in *Psychology Today,* "The pain and fear that come with sadomasochistic sex cause the brain to shunt blood flow away from its executive "decision-making" areas (frontal cortex), which results in an altered state of consciousness in both the giver and the receiver. Like autoerotic asphyxiation or cocaine, experiencing fear and pain can heighten sexual gratification, but at some cost."[14]

Again according to an article in *Psychology Today* by Denise Cummins, Ph.D., women who may generally prefer non-dominant, androgynous-type men, often undergo a shift in preference during their menstrual cycles. During that time, fertility-linked traits, like dominance, may become more attractive and they may be more willing to allow behaviors like submission to become part of the dynamic in the relationship.[15]

I would like to see the evolution of women go full cycle, right through to maximized womanhood. The feminist revolution hasn't gone far enough. It got sidetracked into a place it never had to go. Reaching the point of receiving equal pay for equal work did not require us to become stuck in some netherzone of unsatisfactory male cloning – particularly *perverted* male cloning.

Yes, we may be more independent and better paid at this point in history, but we could have achieved the same thing by maintaining our femininity as real women who won't tolerate the advertising and pornography that demeans us and puts our children at risk.

---

14. *Psychology Today* article by Denise Cummins Ph.D., Feb. 16, 2015

15. *Psychology Today* article by Denise Cummins Ph.D., Feb. 16, 2015

Far Beyond a Public Health Hazard

By the 1980s, the effects on society were disproving the validity of the 1970 Presidential Commission that had declared pornography to be harmless. Child pornography had become unimaginably shocking to the uninitiated. C. Everett Koop was then Surgeon General of the United States. He warned that to ignore the evidence would be to make a conscious decision *not* to see pornography as a clear symptom of stress and disorder. He spoke of its "persistent presence" in four areas of human health:

1. "First there is the field of sexual dysfunction. Pornography intervenes in normal sexual relationships and alters them in some way.

2. "Second, one of the more disturbing pieces of information from our National Centre for Health statistics is the rising rate of suicide among young people. Recently, a number of these suicides were judged to be unintentional, the results of certain auto-erotic behaviors in which soft-core pornographic materials apparently played a significant role.

3. "Third, many women are justifiably concerned about so-called 'copy-cat' rapes. These are rapes that follow the pattern or 'story-line,' if you will, of a rape shown in a pornographic magazine or dramatized on videotape.

4. "Finally...the effects upon individual children are profoundly harmful in physical, psychological and emotional terms. We suspect that the child who survives being used in this way may never again be able to function in normal human relationships. Tragically, some children do not even survive."[16]

16. Minnery, Tom (1986). Pornography: A Human Tragedy, Wheaton, Illinois: Tyndale House Publishers p.107-108.

At that point, while few studies had been done, speculation was rife that society was playing with a python.

Just before the Internet became common in homes, there was hope that children's advocates were beginning to rein in the child porn problem. At that time, it was thought that about 300 children were being victimized.[17]

But then the python wrapped its slimy cords around the world and began its slow squeeze against the breath of innocence.

Porn use is not just a matter of psychological damage and adverse effects on relationships. It can lead to serious health consequences, as reported by Allison Pearson, a columnist for *The Telegraph*, London:

"I was having dinner with a group of women when the conversation moved on to how we could raise happy, well-balanced sons and daughters who are capable of forming meaningful relationships when internet pornography has changed the landscape of adolescence beyond recognition...

"A GP, let's call her Sue, said: 'I'm afraid things are much worse than people suspect.' In recent years, Sue had treated growing numbers of teenage girls with internal injuries caused by frequent anal sex; not, as Sue found out, because they wanted to, or because they enjoyed it, but because a boy expected them to. 'I'll spare you the gruesome details,' said Sue, 'but these girls are very young and slight and their bodies are simply not designed for that.'

"Her patients were deeply ashamed at presenting with such injuries. They had lied to their mums about it and felt they couldn't confide in anyone else, which only added to their distress. When Sue questioned them further, they said they were humiliated by the experience

17. Margaret Sullivan, The Buffalo News, Oct. 21, 2007.

but they had simply not felt they could say no. Anal sex was standard among teenagers now, even though the girls knew it hurt.... The girls presenting with incontinence were often under the age of consent and from loving, stable homes. Just the sort of kids who, two generations ago, would have been enjoying riding and ballet lessons, and still looking forward to their first kiss, not being coerced into violent sex by some kid who picked up his ideas about physical intimacy from a dogging video on his mobile. ...more than four in 10 girls between 13 and 17 in England say they have been coerced into sex acts, according to one of the largest European polls on teenage experiences. Research by the universities of Bristol and Central Lancashire concluded that a fifth of girls had suffered violence or intimidation from teenage boyfriends, a high proportion of whom regularly viewed pornography, with one in five harbouring 'extremely negative attitudes towards women.'

"The end result is what Sue sees as a GP. Young girls – children, really – who abase themselves to pass for normal in a grim, pornified culture. According to another study of British teenagers, most youngsters' first experience of anal sex occurred within a relationship, but it was 'rarely under circumstances of mutual exploration of sexual pleasure.' Instead, it was boys who pushed the girls to try it, with boys reporting that they felt 'expected' to take that role. Moreover, both genders expected males to find pleasure in the act whereas females were mostly expected to "endure the negative aspects such as pain or a damaged reputation."[18]

Allison concluded her article by saying, "However embarrassing it may be, we need to educate and embolden our daughters to fight back against pornography, which is warping the behaviour of boys who are supposed to be their lovers, not their abusers."

---

18 London Telegraph columnist Allison Pearson in The Canberra Times, April, 2015

Cruelty and humiliation are replacing intimacy, friendship and love as the elements young people are learning about relationships. Depiction of these elements is the theme of today's pornography, taking us far beyond issues of public health hazards.

With digital cameras and the Internet, photos of a new child being abused can go around the world in seconds. Computer hard drives can now store more video footage and images of child sexual abuse than any porn magazine library. With everything happening so fast, the unquenchable appetites of perverts for more and more new material is creating a demand for more and more shocking images. Thus, the age of children in the material is decreasing and the level of sadism depicted is increasing. Now the number of children being victimized as subjects of pornography is thought to be upwards of 100,000 worldwide.[19]

Deepening the victimization of the children used in this material is the fact that once the images of their abuse are posted on the web, they are in permanent circulation. No matter whether the children are rescued or not, the theft of their privacy and innocence continues indefinitely. There is no end to it.

Rosalind Prober, president of Beyond Borders, when interviewed in the Canadian National Post about the arrest of a high-profile predator, said, "There is certainly an element of excitement that comes from the risk factor of sharing the pictures. Part of the sexual high comes from conning people, fooling people. There is some thrill-seeking involved. It is a crime of impulse control, similar to addiction. It is also a case of networking on the Internet and finding a community and getting away with it for a bit and then getting sloppy. They're getting away with it so long they feel immune. It also shows how brazen these people are and how weak our system is for protecting children. It is really only the dumb ones that the police

19. Ibid..

manage to catch, those so sexually obsessed that they take risks that expose them. The smartest and most sophisticated ones are very much out there."

Just because someone is not into child porn does not mean they won't molest a child. Any kind of pornography desensitizes a viewer to the humanity of the adults or children used in the images or videos. It's not about the heart or the mind: it's about the thighs, breasts, penises, vaginas, and butts. Skin – anybody's skin – is just the surface of body parts to use for self-gratification.

Pornography as Child Sexual Abuse

People tend to think that premature sexualization of a child happens only with the actual touch of a perpetrator.

Not so. When a child is exposed to pornography, the experience can be so stimulating that it marks the brain. I remember babysitting when I was about twelve years old in a home with vastly different values than those of my parents. After the children were asleep, I pulled a dog-eared movie magazine out of a rack and was shocked by the Frederick's of Hollywood lingerie ads. It was my first exposure to something so explicit and it affected me to the extent that I can still picture the black ads on cheap, yellowish newsprint – 60 years after first seeing them.

If something like a lingerie ad was seared on my brain to the extent that I can still clearly visualize it 60 years later, imagine the effect on a child who gets into someone's hard-core porn stash. Such children can become precociously aroused and begin acting out, perhaps with a younger sibling, thus perpetrating the sexual abuse.

Irresponsible parents who allow the possibility of such an intro-duction to pornography become complicit in the inappropriate sexualization of children. In the same way, when they "normalize" or display their own sexual behavior in the home, they are forcing their children to assess a type of activity the human brain is not yet meant to process at that stage of development. The result can be actual brain damage and inappropriate acting out (see Booklet #8 in this *Predator-Proof Your Family Series – It's All About the Brain*).

More Links Between Child Sexual Abuse and Pornography

In January of 1989, Ted Bundy, America's notorious serial killer, engaged in his last television interview. He credited his progressive use of pornography with having led him to sexually mutilate and kill at least thirty women. He told Dr. James Dobson how, at the age of twelve, he had begun to indulge in the kind of "soft-core" porn available at corner stores. He said, "Like an addiction, you keep craving something which is harder, something which gives you a greater sense of excitement until you reach the point where the pornography only goes so far. You reach that jumping-off point where you're beginning to wonder if maybe actually doing it would give you that which is beyond just reading about or looking at it."

The psychiatrist who was hired by Bundy's lawyers, later revealed that his first exposure to pornography came as a preschooler. His grandfather kept a stash hidden in their greenhouse, and little Ted would sneak out there and look at the pictures.

In the interview, Bundy told how, just as his appetite for pornography was progressive, his murderous crimes began with peeping in windows and stalking women.

According to the latest research findings, use of pornography by sex offenders appears to be a major cause of sex crimes.

Clifford Olson, the worst serial killer Canada has ever known, violently murdered eleven children over nine months in 1980-1981. Two years before his killing spree, the police in Sydney, Nova Scotia, found pornographic pictures of young children in his luggage.

Story after story recounts the same progression of involvement with pornography where the photographs feed and legitimize deviant sexuality. With the mushrooming quantity of pornography, increased numbers of studies by social scientists have shown that such material has a negative effect on many who view it.

One of the best-known studies on the correlation between the availability of pornography and the rate of sexual assault was undertaken in Denmark. When the Copenhagen police and other researchers examined the data, they found clear evidence that violent sexual assaults had increased markedly in the subsequent years.

When South Australia loosened its constraints on pornography, the number of rapes rose sixfold.

Sociologists at the University of New Hampshire compared the sales of corner-store pornography with the crime rate in each state. They found a high correlation between pornography sales and incidents of sexual assaults.

Are You Raising a Child Molester?

Every child molester was raised by someone. Sick people who molest children don't just suddenly appear, having stepped off the go-train from Mars. They are born into people groups, usually families, who are expected to guide them into healthy adulthood.

While healthy humans are born with the propensity to engage in sexual activity, they're not born to be pedophiles or child molesters.

Those desires are developed as a result of early experiences or interruptions in normal development.

Everyone needs to be touched and loved and given attention. As individuals mature, sexual satisfaction is added to the list of needs. During puberty, boys suddenly become preoccupied with sex. Their sex hormones increase fivefold within a two year period. Whatever sexual messages are delivered to them during that period are naturally going to have great significance. If they have normal interactions with females during that time, they are more likely to develop as heterosexuals.

On the other hand, if they are socially awkward and experience sexual arousal with the same sex or with someone considerably younger, it will be remembered as pleasurable, and they may begin to seek out that source of arousal again and again, rather than changing the brain cues and seeking satisfaction from the healthy source.

Parents and guardians have more of a shot at preventing the development of another predator than any politician, teacher or social worker. The home can be the germinating environment for either a healthy son or daughter – or a predator.

Force yourself to imagine walking down a long, concrete hall, pushing a buzzer at a door, entering a room lined with windowed stalls equipped with telephone receivers – and seeing your son (or daughter) in an orange jumpsuit on the other side of a window, waiting to talk to you via one of the receivers.

All your early hopes and early dreams for your child die right there as you are smacked hard by a smirking reality. Totally at the mercy of the guards and other inmates, in a world that doesn't care what kind of a big shot you are or what kind of a home your child comes from, he (or she) hangs his head on the other side of the glass. There sits the embodiment of all the efforts, money and time you have, or have not, poured into him.

You stare, remembering all the violent, sex-laced video games you allowed him to play. A scene of life-like figures gang-raping a female on his monitor snaps across your mind. You remember the hours he spent alone at his computer while you zoned out in front of the television after a long day at the office. You remember the first time he found your stash of porn and how embarrassed you were by his questions.

You knew he didn't like himself very much, but you thought his aggressive behavior with younger children would fix itself. You remember the first time you found him logging on to porn sites and wish now that you had taken the time to figure out what to say to him. You remember all those times you closed the door behind you, off to another event while your child was left to his own devices.

Until faced with it in our own homes, we think of sex-offenders as anonymous faces splashed across the daily news. We suppose they were raised in some shapeless void from which they simply emerged as fully-ripened predators.

The reality is that child molesters are all born as sweet babies. Their lives are blank slates upon which we as parents and guardians get to write. While some circumstances may be beyond our control, the truth is that the more diligently we parent, the more accountability we require, the more positive goals and purposes we establish, the more we show them how important they are to us, the less likelihood we have of hearing the awful news one day, that they have sexually assaulted someone; the less likelihood of having to walk down that long, lonely hallway.

As parents, we have a choice: we can bring cute babies into the world and spend eighteen busy years focussing on building enjoyable children who will contribute to life – or – we can bring cute babies into the world and leave them to their own devices while we do our own thing – and then spend the rest of our lives in misery, wishing we could redo those critical eighteen years.

A September 20, 2017, report by The London Daily Mail should serve as a splash of cold water on parents who aren't paying attention to what their kids are watching. It claims that porn has fueled a 400 percent rise in child-on-child assaults in the UK. "Convictions of rape by those aged under 17 have almost doubled there in just four years. A representative from the country's Ministry of Justice has warned that extreme pornography is fueling this alarming rise in the number of child rapists.

"Experts say violent pornography is influencing children to act out the aggressive, hard core scenes they see online. For example, a couple of weeks ago, an 11-year-old boy admitted seven counts of rape and sexual assault on boys under 13 after he watched similar explicit images online. Legal officials involved in the case said it was clear that Internet porn had sparked the sex attacks.

"Statistics published by the UK's Ministry of Justice revealed 120 children were convicted of rape in 2015, the last figures that are available. That was a 74 percent rise, up from 69 convictions in 2011. Of the 120 children convicted of rape, 46 were sentenced to detention and 61 received community orders. The remaining 13 were dealt with in other ways. Average custodial sentence? 44 months.

"In response to the huge spike in child-on-child attacks, Justice Minister Phillip Lee highlighted his concerns recently at a youth justice conference. 'We are seeing an Internet age driving greater access to more worrying imagery online,' said Lee. 'In the extreme [images], the sexualization of youth is manifesting itself in younger conviction ages for rape.'"

Porn is the new sex education for countless children across the world. For many, it's their first exposure to sex, and that's a huge problem because of what they're learning.

The National Society for the Prevention of Cruelty to Children (NSPCC) recently conducted a survey in the UK of more than 1,000 children aged 11-16 and found that at least half had been exposed to online porn. Of this group, 94 percent have seen it by age 14.

In the same survey, many boys revealed that they wanted to copy the behavior they had seen watching porn. More than a third of 13 – 14-year-olds and a fifth of 11 to 12-year-olds wanted to repeat porn acts. These answers came despite more than three-quarters of the kids agreeing that porn didn't help them understand consent.

One of the most unsettling findings from the NSPCC survey was that over half of the boys (53 percent) believed that what they view in porn is an accurate depiction of sex and sexuality. Thirty-nine percent of girls believed the same.

Do these figures not scream a warning that it is more important than ever for parents and guardians to educate young people about sexual matters and the unrealities of pornography? What these children are learning from porn are skewed perceptions of sex and harmful attitudes about how to treat others, to say the least. The digital age is bringing exponential new threats to children. We must stop underestimating the harms of porn and reach out to educate those around us.

The Internet is worldwide. And porn is fuelled increasingly by the Internet. And kids are kids around the world.

Who the Heck Looks at Child Pornography?

Sitting alone in his tidy, second-story apartment, a thirty-something man listens to his latest CD and peers into his computer monitor, his freshly manicured hands directing the content on his screen. A screaming toddler is being raped, pleading for help. He watches, mesmerized, addicted to his revulsion. When that video ends, he prowls around the sites for even more graphic material. Who is this man and why is he on our planet?

David G. Heffler is a Lockport psychotherapist who is appointed by the courts to counsel child pornography offenders and has seen men from many different walks of life. In an article in the Buffalo News, he said that men who watch child pornography usually fall into one of two categories:

- Hard-core pedophiles and molesters who use child pornography to indulge their fantasies (and seduce their victims)
- Men who start out looking at adult pornography but then "slide down a slippery slope" towards child pornography

"Many men told me they started out looking at adult porn and never intended to look at children, but after looking at adult porn for a long time, they get bored. They want to try something different. They start looking at children. Then, they can't get enough of it."[20]

The usual responses these men give when asked why they look at child pornography include depression, drunkenness or their own issues arising from having been molested as children themselves.

A recent study by the U.S. Federal Bureau of Prisons[21] reported that

20. Michel, Lou and Herbeck, Dan, *Confessions of a Child Porn Addict*, The Buffalo News, Oct. 21, 2007

21 Michel, Lou and Herbeck, Dan, *Confessions of a Child Porn Addict*, The Buffalo News, Oct. 21, 2007

80 percent of the convicts studied who look at child pornography, acknowledged that they molested children – even if they were never charged with the crime.

The U.S. National Center for Missing and Exploited Children studied 1,713 people charged with possessing child pornography, 96 percent of whom were convicted. Almost all were male. Ninety-one percent were white. Forty-nine percent were sent to prison. Seventy-three percent had never been arrested for a sexual offense. Eighty-three percent had images of children aged six to twelve and 19 percent had images of children under the age of three. Thirty-eight percent were married or were in stable relationships and 46 percent had access to minors at home or work or through activities. Sixty-two percent had pictures of girls. Here's the worst – 80 percent had images showing the sexual penetration of a child.

From Statistics to Real People

Behind every number added to a statistic, lies a real person.

Recently, a national newspaper printed an open letter from a man convicted and awaiting sentencing for viewing child pornography. The writer's purpose was to warn others what would happen to them if they, too, were discovered possessing child pornography.

He told of the sudden terror of having his home raided by 10 FBI agents who burst in and separated him and his innocent wife for full interrogation in separate bedrooms. Led away from his upscale home in handcuffs, he was further interrogated at the FBI center and was placed in a dingy cell with nothing but a cot and a toilet. Before being sent home to await a court appearance, he was called before a judge, instructed to retain a lawyer, photographed, fingerprinted and fitted with an electronic monitoring system for which he has to pay a

$100.00 monthly rental fee. When he called his boss to let him know what had happened, he lost his position, his income and his respect in the business world.

He spoke of the devastation of not being allowed to be alone with his grandchildren, of his nine o'clock curfew, of his loss of freedom to travel, of giving up his passport, of being barred from voting and coaching children's sports, of being rejected from his club memberships and of being unable to winter with his wife in the south.

This man knows the likelihood that he faces prison time and it frightens him. The last sentence of his letter is a warning to readers that if they indulge in watching child pornography, they will regret not paying attention to his message.

Interview With a Predator – the Husband I Never Knew

When I published the first edition of this *Predator-Proof Your Family* series of nine booklets, I did not publish from the personal perspective of the ex-wife of a child-molester. I wanted to protect my family from any unwanted public glare. In the seven intervening years, I have come to understand that the silence was not doing my precious family any favors. Silence is the favorite place of hiding for predators. They count on victims being too ashamed to release the deep dark secret. My family and I bear no shame. The shame belongs to the perpetrator. We were all victims. Our strength lies in our voice.

My grandchildren and great-grandchildren need to know that they do not bear the name of a child molester, but that their name has been redeemed through helping other families to escape the destructive fruit of pornography. While I have forgiven (*not condoned!*) my ex-husband (in terms of not being bound up in bitterness) and we have moved on with our lives in opposite directions, I will not model silence for victims who need to find their voices and get help.

40

Life did not have to end this way. Early on in our relationship, prior to the advent of the Internet, when I discovered that my husband was into pornography, it became a huge problem because it made me feel inadequate as a woman – as though I wasn't 'enough' for him. Any sense of security in our relationship was dissolved in fears that he was finding pictures of other naked women more attractive than I. I felt devalued and objectified because my "competition" was a one-dimensional image on a glossy page, rendering personal relationship meaningless. There was no way I could compete. No one air-brushed me the way they did the "other" women.

Discussions led to promises that he would stop buying and indulging in porn. But then I would be making the bed and find things tucked between the mattresses – or be taking bathroom curtains down to wash and discover pornographic novels resting on top of the window-frame, supported by the curtains.

On the day the novels fell into the bathtub, I flipped one open and read a page. Despite the fact that that was 47 years ago, I can still remember the scenario detailed on that page, because it was so horrifying that it burned itself onto my brain. I confronted my husband and asked where he had purchased such disgusting material. Surprisingly, he told me that he'd gotten the books at a particular convenience store in the Ontario town where we were then living.

I was not happy. At that time, my first baby boy was about three months old. I put him, in his little blue onesie, in his car seat and drove to the store. Sure enough, there was a whole rack of gross material there. I purchased one and drove to the police station. Book in hand, I carried my little boy up the concrete steps and asked to see the chief. A woman ushered me into his office.

A round-faced man in a too-tight uniform looked up from a mess of papers. I placed my son, still in his car seat, on top of the papers, directly facing him. As the chief looked from me to my baby, I tossed the book on his desk beside the car seat. Remember – I was not happy.

The first words spoken were mine. "How," I asked, "do you expect me to raise this child to be a man of integrity and honor when his father can purchase garbage like this in your town?"

The chief picked up the novel, looked first at the front cover and then at the back, fanned through the pages, stuttered some less-than-memorable words and mumbled something about "looking into it." I later discovered that he, himself, was a big user of pornography.

Years of the absence of signs of pornography in our home were followed by intermittent discoveries of evidence that we still had a problem. In those days, I didn't understand the issue of addiction or anything about physical changes in the brain.

Unbeknownst to me, the addiction had devolved into deeper and deeper perversions until, one day, an opportunity presented itself and all my husband's stored and multiplied fantasies ripened into the molestation of a young girl. The instant that he touched her, changed her life and the course of the lives of our entire family. In that moment, he became a child molester – a criminal – and lived with his secret for 25 years.

By the mid 90's, it appeared to me that pornography had disappeared from our lives. Little did I know that everything had changed with the advent of the Internet, and magazines and novels had been replaced by the click of a mouse.

It was only when one of the victims dared to break the silence that, after a week of disbelief, I discovered that the porn had never gone away. It had simply gone underground.

Despite the charges, my trust in my husband had grown to the point that, even when I was put in the position of having to believe either him or the victim who had spoken out, I believed his plea of not guilty – from the Monday he was charged, until his confession on Friday. No matter my love for both, I had to choose the one I trusted most. Weighing the trust that had finally grown over 38 years of marriage against a beloved teenager who could have many factors influencing her charges, I made the wrong choice; a choice that remains. one of the biggest regrets of my life. It made life so much more difficult for everyone.

So convinced was I of his innocence, that I booked a lie detector test to prove it to everyone. I could hardly wait for the Sunday appointment to arrive. Feigning agreement that it was a good idea, he knew that every day brought him closer to exposure. He finally confessed, and the world, as we then knew it, blew up. The ground between us opened up and gave way to an uncrossable gulf.

He was convicted, imprisoned – and divorced. When he was released from prison, he was genuinely remorseful and wanted to cooperate with any efforts to warn people about the dangers of pornography – and hopefully prevent others from letting it grow into the crime that shattered our family and his victims. When I asked if he would consent to an interview for this series, he agreed without hesitation. The full interview can be found here and there throughout the series, in segments pertaining to the topic of the particular booklet.

D. When did you first get into pornography?

W. When I was a teenager, I went to work for a summer for my uncle in New York. I had my first car, and I remember going into a corner store there and buying some novels that were very pornographic.

D. What led you to those books?

W. It was just curiosity at first and then sexual excitement and sexual gratification with masturbation. That kind of thing.

D. *Did those novels contain pornographic material about children?*

W. Not at first, but later on I did come across storylines that involved children, often in incestuous kinds of circumstances.

D. *You've been talking about pornographic novels. When did you start into magazines?*

W. About the same time. The novels were cheaper.

D. *Did you find that as you got into porn, there was a desire for more and more explicit material?*

W. Yes, although I never got into child pornography, other than what I came across by accident in those early novels.

D. *You stopped using pornography for awhile. How did you get involved again?*

W. With the Internet. I saw some pop-ups and got curious and found there was tons of it.

D. *How did you hide that from me?*

W. Well, I just didn't go online when you were at home. I'd wait until you went out and then I'd get into it.

D. *What would you say to someone who was on the edge, was fooling around with pornography, hadn't touched a child yet, but was fantasizing about doing it? Knowing what you know now, what warning could you give potential molesters that could deter them from sexually interfering with a child?*

W. It's a tough situation because, from a self-preservation standpoint, there's nowhere for the potential perpetrator to go without severe repercussions. If he hasn't touched a child yet, there hasn't been any law broken, but to go to anyone to discuss it, he would have to be very careful that it was the right person. But the reality is that if you do it, you're eventually going to get caught. Look at all these old priests, 70 and 80 years old who thought they'd gotten away with it all those years...but then the victims started to tell.

D. *What if they've already molested a child?*

W. If something has actually happened, people who know about it are bound by law to identify predators, and predators have to come to the conclusion that they will have to accept the consequences. There's no way around that. They will have to pay the price, one way or another.

The thing is that if you've done something, in the grand scheme of things, you want to hope that you get caught on this side of eternity. If it doesn't come out until the other side, there's no chance to make anything right, and you'll have to suffer in torment forever. You're done. There is no hope. Ever. You've got to get help. You've got to stop.

The good thing about facing the music, if there is a good part, is that they can stop themselves from hurting another child and have a second chance at changing who they are. For those who want to rebuild their lives and change, there's a good possibility that they may find a support group and the respect of mature people who will nurture them along in their battle.

I'm a living testament to that. As you know, I went from having a nice middle-class life with all the amenities; you know, a great family, nice cars, big house, a half-decent business that kept us going for many years – to absolutely nothing.

But I'm better now than I was with all that because with a strong support group, I'm finally living an honest life.

I went to the first job I could find after getting out of prison as a night watchman for a trucking company. I did well – got a raise far before I was supposed to get a raise. Then they found out I'd been in prison and boom. They let me go. I was emotionally devastated.

If molesters turn themselves in, eventually they have to realize that there is a segment of society that will never forgive them, no matter how well they try to do. There are those that already have and there are those who may eventually be able to.

But until something actually happens, there's still the chance of getting help. If I had known the pastor I have now, I could have talked to him.

D. Would you have?

W. Most likely not. In all honesty, probably not. But I could have because he's a guy you could reach out to who would make you accountable and get you help. And that's what you need. You can't just think, well I'm going to fix this because you can't.

With all the therapy I've had now, I've found that there's a lot of secular garbage out there that just doesn't work. Undoubtedly it does help some people, but it's all about self-help, and that doesn't always work because sometimes you need help beyond yourself. So-called fixes are all over the map. Some will tell you that pornography is a good thing, that it helps you get release – get into it so that you don't molest someone...but it's like – hello.

D. These are treatment places that are telling you this?

W. Well you know there are some that say, "Why don't you just go and get release with some porn instead of molesting a child?" That mindset is out there, and it's perpetrated by the porn industry, because it's a multi-billion dollar industry and that's the bottom line. The buck. And it's not just sleazebags producing it. Media conglomerates that everyone thinks of as reputable are bankrolling these things. Listen to the lyrics on MTV. I'd name the sponsors, but everybody knows who they are anyway. This is the stuff kids are feeding on.

D. So you would not have gotten help without getting caught.

W. I don't think so.

On a very personal level, I wondered for many years why W. seemed uninterested in sex. When I asked him – numerous times – he always responded that he guessed he just didn't have a very high sex drive. Reasonably satisfied that it wasn't anything I was doing wrong, I accepted his answer.

It wasn't until after his conviction and this subsequent interview, that he admitted he had had no appetite for normal sex. The pornography had perverted his appetites to the extent that anything less than the kind of activity he could watch online was not interesting to him.

Thirty-eight lonely years. Robbed. More than robbed. Addiction to pornography stole not only our 38 years of intimacy but the childhoods of his victims, our family, the lives we should have had...and on it goes. And what did it profit him? He was like a prince who sold his kingdom for a bag of snakes.

While W. was never into images of child pornography, his sex addiction gave him a desire for illicit sex – whether with a child or an adult. It was about whoever was available. The very nature of pornography gradually leads viewers into wanting more and more explicit or unnatural material. Once whetted, the appetite for obscene images is insatiable. It's like a black hole that can never be filled. Had W. not been found out, images of child pornography would no doubt have become part of it all.

Letter From A Sex Offender:
How I Went From Vanilla Porn To Child Porn[22]

Many people contact "Fight the New Drug" to share their personal stories about how porn has affected their lives or the life of a loved one. The following personal account demonstrates the damage that pornography does to real lives and how a seemingly harmless habit can get completely out of control and escalate into more extreme, darker territories – sometimes to material that is considered taboo or violent, sometimes moving on to content that is illegal.

"It might surprise you to know I am a sex offender. My crime was downloading indecent images of children on the Internet for which I was arrested, and it's something I'm deeply ashamed of, but my story starts long before I progressed on to that kind of content.

"I was 15 when I had my first taste of Internet porn; this was back in the day of the dial-up modem. I'm 33 now, and my life panned out like a lot of others who became hooked on easy to access pornography. Having a PC in my bedroom from the time I was 16-years-old didn't help, and that's when I started collecting porn. All legal "vanilla" porn back then.

"I grew up through most of my adult life consuming porn, yet my sex life in the physical world was woefully inadequate, and I was always painfully shy around girls. I did have a relationship once for five years, but it's been over ten years since I've experienced real intimacy. I realize now that my habits around the consumption of

22. From September 20, 2017 "Fight the New Drug." www.fightthenewdrug.org

48

porn, instead of improving my sex life, actually helped build a wall between me and intimacy.

"Moving on to after I finished University, I had some trauma to deal with regarding the loss of my mother to cancer and my grandfather the year after that. It was a difficult time, and I chose the wrong way of dealing with it. I gave in to the temptation of cocaine, and still having a compulsive porn habit, I used the drugs to get an increased high while viewing it, and my tastes changed over time to more extreme content…which led to my inevitable arrest.

"Today I am over two years sober from alcohol, cannabis, cocaine, and porn! Thanks to the 12 steps and the help of other recovering addicts, and I intend to stay that way.

"I've spent a lot of time doing research about the effects of pornography, and I knew this was the foundation of my problem. When I started to understand the model of desensitization, the accessibility, affordability and anonymity factors and started reading about other people's experiences, I realized I had a problem with online porn.

"I felt at odds with people who called me a pedophile because, to put it bluntly, I find women attractive and that's always been my primary focus when thinking about relationships. I started to read accounts from other people who claimed they had an attraction to underage people and I also found that I didn't agree with their views either, to me they just sounded like excuses to continue thinking sick thoughts, like the addict who is in denial and can't see the wood for the trees.

"The thing what helped me most was learning and understanding, getting my emotions back after experiencing sobriety and realizing that I did have empathy and I am human after all. It's that empathy now which makes me feel like people need to be educated about the dangers of porn because time and again it has been shown to encourage criminal behavior and add to mental health problems.

"I never had a 'talk' about porn growing up and my parents always neatly avoided the subject with me, so my education about sex, love, and intimacy was garnered from porn and the abusive narratives that go along with it."

The Pornography Prescription:
Why Are Therapists Advising Patients To Watch Porn?[23]

When I first heard about sex therapists recommending commercial pornography to their patients, I was stunned. To me, it was like a doctor treating an alcoholic with shots of whiskey – or cocaine addicts being given cocaine. Excuse me?

Nevertheless, certain kinds of sex therapy and pornography seem to have a long history of mutual dependence.

To me, it's a no-brainer that a model of sex advice that promotes the basis of struggle and has been proven to be destructive to the development and preservation of recognizably healthy[24] relationships needs to be questioned. The recognition of harms associated with pornography production and consumption is growing. Any such prescription is lacking in understanding of the roots of the problem.

Ever since the founding of modern sex therapy techniques in the 1960's, from the work of Masters and Johnson, the pornography and

---

23. Adapted from an article by Meagan Tyler, a Research Fellow at RMIT University. Original headline: "A prescription for porn: should sex therapists recommend pornography to patients?"

24. While some might question my use of the adjective "healthy" as subjective, the reality is that society needs plumblines or standards of decency, just as there has to be a recognized set of rules for driving cars on highways. According to Dictionary.com, *"Wholesome has connotations of attractive freshness and purity; it applies to what is good for one, physically, morally, or both*: wholesome food; wholesome influences or advice."

sex therapy industries have been linked. Incredibly, they used pornography in the training of therapists, in diagnostic work, and often in treatment.

They went from attempting to change the sexual responses of gay men by depriving them of water for 18 hours after watching films of gay sex and giving drinks contingent on increased erection response after being shown heterosexual pornographic imagery – to using pornography to "treat" sexual dysfunctions for women having trouble engaging in sex with their male partners. The idea was that these women could be encouraged to participate in sex by being shown pornographic films while practicing relaxation techniques.

In using pornography in the treatment of child molesters, arousal is measured in response to a variety of stimuli, supposedly to determine what "turns patients on." One has to question why the focus could not be turned to constructive, healthy activities, rather than subjecting the patient to the very thing that caused the problem in the first place, thereby driving the obsession deeper.

A 2016 collection of thoughts by Heather Brunskell-Evans, *The Sexualized Body and the Medical Authority of Pornography*, "examines pornography as a material practice that eroticizes gender inequality and sexual violence towards women. It addresses the complex relationship between pornography and medicine (in particular, sexology and psycho-therapy) whereby medicine has historically, and currently, afforded pornography considerable legitimacy and even authority. Pornography naturalizes women's submission and men's dominance as if gendered power is rooted in biology, not politics. In contrast to the populist view that medicine is objective and rational, the contributors here demonstrate that medicine has been complicit with the construction of gender difference, and in that construction, the relationship with pornography is not incidental but fundamental.[25]" The collection demonstrates that there is practically no evidence to support the efficacy of pornography in treatments. Nevertheless, a lack of evidence has not halted its use.

In a 2008 study, around a third of sex therapists in the USA reported using pornography, even when that was specifically defined as involving violent, dehumanizing or sexist content. They tended to cite education and desensitization as primary justifications for its use, despite concerns that it normalizes violent and degrading material.

Eighty-eight percent of scenes in popular pornography contain acts of physical aggression, with the targets being "overwhelmingly" female. It makes no sense that women are being told that this is a normal model of sexuality they should emulate.

Porn "actresses" are paid to fake their sexual enjoyment. Do the therapists not think women are aware of the unreality of it all? But when a troubled woman sits across from a qualified therapist who claims to have the experience, the results and the answers, the power dynamics of therapy can be intimidating.

Female-friendly pornography? What even is that? I know it sounds like bad grammar - but what even is that?

With the lack of evidence of any value in using pornography as treatment, and with a growing recognition of the harms associated with it, it's hard to understand why this practice has been allowed to continue for so long. Who benefits from it? It all comes down to the buck, after all.

Alyssa Friedman-Yan, a licensed New York City based therapist, said it has become common for the therapeutic community to meet

25. From the Amazon.com synopsis

individuals or couples seeking treatment for either addiction to, or problems in partner relations related to Internet porn. "As people are able to access and watch such a variety of extreme sexual activity, this can affect the actual act of 'standard/vanilla' sexual activity with partners," she said.

Pornography as a "Grooming" Tool

In the intro, I mentioned the old deep-south slavery that was challenged and defeated by brave freedom advocates of the day – but how about 21st-century slavery in North America – and all around the world?

One of the most disturbing elements of the use of pornography today is its use for desensitizing children who are about to be abused and children / teens who are being sex-trafficked.

In *Booket #2* of this *Predator-Proof Your Family Series*, in identifying danger signs of predators, I wrote about the "grooming" process, or the process of preparing a child to be abused and gaining the trust of his or her guardians or parents to get the needed access to the child.

Predators often use their collections of erotica and pornography to show to their victims as part of the grooming process of seduction. They think that when their victims see the photographs, their inhibitions will be lowered and they'll be more inclined to accept sexual activity as something people normally do.

"Over two-thirds of all calls to the National Human Trafficking Resource Center involve sex trafficking – an estimated 21 million victims worldwide[26] – with 49 percent of all trafficking victims and

---

26. University Of New England, "Human Sex Trafficking: An Online Epidemic #Infographic" (2015). Retreived By Http://Www.Visualistan.Com/2015/02/Human-Sex-Trafficking-Online-Epidemic.Html

70 percent of underage trafficking victims reporting that pornography was made of them while they were enslaved.[27]"

Without going into how these children and teens are procured, every day, in towns and cities all across North America (and worldwide), vans with blacked/whited-out windows transport kids from town to town to serve the horrendous appetites of adults for perverted sex. They don't keep the kids in any one town too long, for fear they'll be recognized or removed from captivity.

Some use photographs and videos they have made of their victims to blackmail them into further sexual activity. After victims are ensnared, porn is often used to desensitize them to the acts in which they will be forced to engage.

Porn facilitates human trafficking, and human trafficking feeds porn.

Pornography as 21st-Century Board Games

The hell of pornography in the 21st-century is too dehumanizing to describe – and yet it's portrayed every day, with clicks of mice in the hands of kids and family members, the way we used to roll the dice for Snakes and Ladders. Suffice it to say that when you have entertainment software companies developing life-like graphics that people can manipulate on the screen, undressing them, shackling and raping them, all to accompanying associated sounds, society has a problem. We need to wake up.

In 1992, when researchers found games like "Mortal Kombat" to be harmful to developing minds, the United States government formed the Entertainment Software Rating Board (ESRB) to deal with the

27. Thorn, "A Report On The Use Of Technology To Recruit, Groom, And Sell Domestic Minor Sex Trafficking Victim (2015). Retrieved From Https://Www.Wearethorn.Org/Wp-Content/Uploads/2015/02/Survivor_Survey_r5.Pdf

concerns. It designated particularly gruesome games with a "Mature" rating and worked with some success until apathy, and parental pre-occupation replaced efficacy.

The problem is that video game violence differs from other kinds of media, like reading, where the reader is a passive participant. With interactive video games, the player takes an active role. While it's true that not all who play these games become clones of the lifelike graphics, encouraging a player to perpetrate violent acts can normalize violence in a culture already too accepting of it. People who haven't been on the wrong end of violence don't understand how much it hurts. Nevertheless, most M-rated action games glorify war, killing, and violence (whether or not it involves sex) as if they are "fun." What they really are, are tools of abuse.

We can't think it's okay for a teenage boy – or girl – to play these "games" for a couple of hours and then ride his or her bike around the streets with the neighborhood children. A perversion-soaked mind is an assault waiting to happen.

"Call of Duty" allows players to take on the role of blood thirsty soldiers, arming themselves with an arsenal of weapons including rifles, pistols, and grenades. Norwegian mass killer Anders Breivik claimed he had trained himself to kill his 77 victims through playing the game.

In March of 2015, a letter was sent by a group of schools in Cheshire, UK regarding concerns about the "levels of violence and sexual content" to which young people were being exposed with games such as "Call of Duty," "Grand Theft Auto," "Dogs of War" and other similar games renowned for their violent characters. Despite the fact that they may have an 18 classification, classifications don't mean much when kids aren't supervised by diligent parents. The school board claimed these were all inappropriate for children and that they should not have access to them.

It warned that if teachers became aware that any pupils were playing these video games, they would contact police and social services. The Nantwich Education Partnership said that allowing children to play games, such as "Call of Duty," is "neglectful" and puts the children at risk. Why is every school board in the civilized world not following suit?

In 2014, "Grand Theft Auto," the violent bestselling video game franchise, "upgraded" its game to allow players to simulate having sex with a prostitute. Not only does it further glorify crime and violence, but the upgraded version enables people to watch as a virtual prostitute performs sex acts on them, moaning throughout the whole degrading scene. How is this an entertainment option for any age of kids? But that's not the only "improvement" provided by the upgrade. It also gives the "players" the ability to gruesomely murder their prostitutes and take back their money and makes for a much more "immersive" experience. While kids begging their parents to buy the game will plead that the sex part is avoidable, it's not an "allowance" issue. What parent ever says to a child, "Yes, you're allowed to participate in the seedy, violent sex aspects of the game"?

The fact that there is no nudity in these sequences is not the issue. The dialogue is graphic enough that there doesn't have to be actual nudity to have the same result. While adults may claim these scenes to be more comical than arousing, children lack the maturity to make such distinctions. The result has proven to be an increased careless sexual activity at a young age, and mental detriments such as addiction or intimacy disorders later in life have increased.

"Grand Theft Auto" is criminally violent. It enables a player to experience killing any civilian, criminal, or police officer they choose and requires them to brutally torture a chosen victim with pliers, electric clamps, and waterboarding. Unbelievably, this "game" is mechanically designed to be fun, even for a seven-year-old. In truth, it's all about acceptance of violence, nullification of empathy, and the desensitization of our children.

No matter the content, apparently, according to Neilsen ratings, "Duty WWII" and "Assassin's Creed Origins" were the most anticipated games for the 2017 holiday season.

Not surprisingly, the prevalence of sex has been sneakily gradual in games over the last decade. Some people understand child sexual abuse to mean physical rape or molestation – but how about the rape or molestation of the mind of someone in developmental years? Should not the developers, retailers, and proponents of these games be thrown in jail as some of the worst abusers of our young people?

The human brain is not fully developed until around the age of 30 when areas of judgment mature. When participation in games of abuse become part of one's developmental process, we cannot pretend to wonder why we have a societal problem.

I am so beyond offended by this game, as a human being. How is it possible that our culture considers this to be okay, to the degree that this is a bestselling video game? Where are the feminist voices speaking out against this kind of objectification and misogyny? Unbelievable evidence of the schizophrenic nature of popularism. When people of any age spend hour upon hour killing people, stealing things, hiring prostitutes, beating women and indulging in violent virtual sex acts, it frays the fabric of what's okay in real life. Allowing such violent images into one's mind embeds them there, and that's not good for anyone, much less the developing mind of a child.

When people spend hour upon hour using their controllers to kill people, steal things, hire prostitutes, and beat women, it begins to blur the edges of what's okay in real life. It desensitizes them to violence. That's why the military uses video games to help soldiers get over the natural human aversion to killing.

Thousands of millennials have found a new way to make a living by establishing their own YouTube channels and enticing subscribers to support them while they demonstrate the games. Naturally, girls get the most interest and make the most money – sometimes at the rate of many thousands of dollars per month. Many of these claim to be ardent feminists, while at the same time allowing themselves to be objectified through a highly sexual presentation and comments from sponsors. They become virtual stars in a virtual world, traveling around the world to game conventions where their "fans" can score photos with them. It's a virtual world, foreign to those who don't understand the concept of virtual reality.

Video games—especially first-person violent video games—do affect us, even if we don't realize it at the time. We can choose what we let into our homes and what we let into our heads.

Virtual Sex

No longer needing to endure the ups and downs of normal relationships as a context for having flesh-and-blood sex, it's now possible for people to don a pair of clunky goggles and pursue the wildest of sexual fantasies in a virtual world. With googles securely in place, they may see a scantily clad man or woman appear to approach, holding their gaze with lust-designed eyes – and then interact according to however the player chooses to direct the controls. No matter how convincing it may appear, however, the figure is just a three-dimensional performer in a 360-degree immersive video.

Part of what separates virtual reality from traditional video is that its experience is designed to be so powerful and immersive that it tricks people into believing they are actually interacting in a simulated world. The porn industry is now offering digitally-connected sex toys (a rapidly growing field known as teledildonics) to sync virtual videos with the physical movements of toys. No physical sensation is out of the realm of possibility.

By 2025, such adult video content is forecast to be a $1 billion business, the third-biggest virtual-reality sector, after video games ($1.4 billion) and NFL-related content ($1.23 billion), according to estimates from Piper Jaffray. According to analyst Gene Munstery, it's the next "mega tech theme" in the U.S., akin to the mobile-phone industry in the early 21st century.

Strangers in porn magazines and videos don't need to be coaxed into the "mood." They don't require time "wasted" on foreplay. Porn is fast food for perverts.

Artificial 'Intelligence' – Artificial Skin

Synthetic sex is a growing problem in our society. Thanks to a link from "Fight the New Drug," I recently saw an interview by co-hosts Phillip Schofield and Holly Willoughby on the British morning show "This Morning," featuring a UK Dad with a life-size, silicone sex doll that hangs out with his wife and kids. This might sound like a creepy plot to a futuristic movie, but this is happening.

Arran Lee Wright, 36, from North Wales, spent about $4,700.00 developing a specialized, hyper-realistic sex robot that he named "Samantha." With his wife standing just off the main set and his sili-cone girlfriend at his side on the sofa, he was interviewed about how he has incorporated this sex machine into their family life.

Here's how the exchange went down:

"It would be quite frightening if a child found that in your wardrobe," co-host Holly said to Arran. "Well, I have two children myself," he said. "And they actually – well, this one's got a family mode." He went on to explain how "Samantha's" specialized mode prevents her making any inappropriate comments at the wrong moment, and that she even tells jokes.

"She can talk about lots of things," Arran said of the doll that is primarily programmed to simulate sex acts. "She can talk about animals, she can talk about philosophy, she can talk about science," he said, patting the doll's hand.

Holly asked Arran, "But at some point, they are going to know eventually that daddy has sex with Samantha and she isn't mummy. Is that not a bit strange?"

Co-founder of a website that sells lifelike sex robots worth thousands of dollars, Arran denied that it was "strange," saying, "A sex robot is not meant to replace people and we're not trying to replace women. It's used as a supplement to help people."

He says that his children, who are five and three, are used to seeing the doll around the house and ask, "Where's Samantha?" when she's not around. She can normally be found sitting on the couch with his children or even riding in the car and is like "a member of the family" according to Arran *and* his wife.

While Arran's wife, Hannah Nguyen, 38, confirmed she was more than happy for the doll to join them in bed, Psychologist Emma Kenny said (on the show) that she believes robots like Samantha could be the death of healthy human relationships. She slammed the idea of sex dolls for objectifying women's bodies.

She said it wasn't "acceptable or healthy" to use the technology in the way that it can replace relationships with simulation.

But synthetic sex is where we've gotten as a society. Is this an extreme case? We'll have to wait and see for a couple of years. When you consider the normalization of sex dolls along with the global normalization and acceptance of porn, who knows? How about Spain's first ever sex-doll brothel? Who could ever have imagined such a thing a few years ago?

There are those who are quick to point out the short-term benefit of having a sex partner who can't disease them...or fight back, but how is that even real sex without some form of relationship? How is that not just "upgraded" masturbation?

Arran contends that dolls can help people, but some experts are warning of the potential catastrophic damage that AI sex dolls could cause. They're concerned that widely available, highly-advanced sex robots could very well encourage even more sexual violence than society could imagine possible.

One such expert, Professor Noel Sharkey, a computer scientist, warns against the troublesome implications of producing such robots in a study he co-authored called "Our Sexual Future With Robots." Sharkey also recently launched the Foundation for Responsible Robotics to keep watch over the potential dangers of sex robots.

According to Sharkey, the argument that sex robots can help people with unconventional or illegal sexual urges is a weak one, and one that will most likely encourage even more sexual violence. He says this in reference to robots already on the market that feature a rape simulation setting.

"The idea is robots would resist your sexual advances so that you could rape them," he told *Business Insider*. "Some people say it's better they rape robots than rape real people. There are other people saying this would just encourage rapists more."

"We can't be okay with technology taking the place of real, healthy human relationships. Whether it's a computer screen or a sex doll, we need to be educated and take a stand for healthy sexuality and human connection that is rooted in authenticity, mutual love, and mutual trust. Science, facts and personal accounts all agree that synthetic sex isn't best. At the end of the day, technology can never take the place of a real relationship rooted in love, trust, and authenticity.[28]"

Sexting

Sexting? What the heck is that? Prior to the advent of the Internet and cell phones, there was no such word. Again – a new element in the process of the pornogrification of society. This one is novel in its degree of any pretense of privacy and its ability to trap unsuspecting users in unimagined consequences.

According to Wikipedia, "Sexting refers to sending, receiving, or forwarding sexually explicit messages, photographs or images, primarily between mobile phones. It may also include the use of a computer or any digital device. The term was first popularized in the early 21st century, and is a portmanteau of sex and texting."

While film cameras often required a dark room to process negatives in traditional processes of creating pornography, modern camera phones can record sexually explicit images and videos in privacy. At a time when hormones are raging, their brains have not yet developed mature reasoning skills, and they find themselves with a heightened opportunity of titillation, many teenagers use the medium of the

---

28. "Fight the New Drug" www.fightthenewdrug.org

text message to exchange messages of a sexual nature.

Sexting rose in popularity with the advent of several direct messaging apps available on smartphones; such as Kik, Snapchat, and WhatsApp. These allow anyone to transmit content over the Internet with anonymity or, in the case of Snapchat, with the security of the photos self-destructing within 10 seconds. Believing it will disappear without consequences, senders feel more secure about sending personally produced sexual content. However, if the images are saved through other photo capturing technology, third-party applications, or simple screenshots by the recipient, they can be distributed, carrying social and legal implications.

A 2009 study claimed that four percent of teens claimed to have sent sexually explicit photos of themselves, while 15 percent claimed to have also received such images.

How things have changed in seven short years.

A 2016 study entitled *Don't Send Me That Pic* conducted by Plan International Australia revealed:

- Seven out of ten young women surveyed agreed that girls are often bullied or sexually harassed online

- 58 percent agreed that girls often receive uninvited or unwanted indecent or sexually explicit material in texts and porn videos.

- 51 percent agreed that girls are routinely pressured to take 'sexy' photos of themselves and share them

- 82 percent believe it is unacceptable for a boyfriend to ask their girlfriend to share naked photos of themselves

- 44 percent do not feel comfortable reporting incidents of abusive online behaviour

Participants in the survey reported that online sexual bullying and harrassment were a normal part of their everyday lives.

Porn-saturated boys routinely pressure girls to provide acts inspired by the porn they consume. Their sexual behaviors are being molded and conditioned by pornography rather than by honorable, engaged parental figures.

While girls suffer under the stress of expectations to become real-life embodiments of the pornography boys have watched, they lack the resources to deal with the harrassment. Their psyches are being twisted to see their bodies as service stations for male gratification. If they don't mirror the images the boys see on their computer screens (which they never can), they feel inadequate. Sex acts like oral sex are expected in exchange for tokens of affection. Requests for pictures of their body parts have become so normal that many girls become resigned to sending them. For many, it's become a normal part of life and they struggle with questions like, "How do I say no without hurting his feelings?"

Tragically, boys often trade the images with their friends and use them as a form of currency that they hold over the girls' heads if there's a bad breakup. Rating systems for girls bodies have become normal. While most girls know they can never compete with the bodies of porn stars, the reality doesn't take away their pressure to try. The stress coming from the threat of public humiliation from their revealing pics has been too much for many young girls to survive. Teen suicide rates keep climbing.

When asked, "How do you know a guy likes you?," an 8th grade girl replied: "He still wants to talk to you after you [give him oral sex]." A male high school student said to a girl: "If you [give me oral sex] I'll give you a kiss."[29]

---

29 Fight the New Drug - Plan Australia/Our Watch report

Creation and distribution of explicit photos of teenagers violates child pornography laws in many areas. Senders may also be charged with distribution of indecent material to a minor. Having to register as a sex offender for life is nowhere on the radar screen of the participants. Child pornography cases involving teen-to-teen sexting have been prosecuted in both Canada and the USA; in Oregon, Virginia, and Nova Scotia at the time of this writing.

The unfounded sense of virtual safety through sexting was exemplified nowhere more clearly than in the recent case of Jeffrey Sandusky, the 41-year-old son of former Penn State University assistant football coach Jerry Sandusky. The dust had hardly settled on the outrage surrounding the senior Sandusky's arrest in a child molestation case that shook not only Penn State, but the entire country six years prior when, in mid-September, 2017, Jeffrey pleaded guilty to charges of pressuring a teenage girl to send him naked photos and asking her teen sister to give him oral sex.

Jeffrey pleaded guilty to all 14 counts, including solicitation of statutory sexual assault and solicitation of involuntary deviate sexual intercourse. The counts included soliciting sex from a child younger than 16 and soliciting child pornography. According to the district attorney's office, he will spend up to eight years in state prison.

This news saddened me on a personal level. A few months after the conviction of the elder Sandusky, I was given the contact info for his wife, Dottie, with a request from a concerned neighbor to share my own story with her as the ex-wife of a convicted child-molester. She, along with five of her six adopted children, were in denial regarding the conviction. The hope was that some of my hard-won insights might be of help. It became obvious, through our correspondence, that Dottie still believed her husband to be innocent.

My question on page 31, "Are you raising a child molester?" would have been too horrendous a possibility for Dottie to contemplate – because it would have been the last thing she would have set out to do and I am not assigning fault to her. I doubt if anyone (except the sickest among us) ever sets out to raise a pedophile – and yet they emerge; but here we are, six years later, reading the sad story of a family that never dealt with the issues of pornography and abuse that finally destroyed them.

There is a tidal wave of new molesters being groomed to abuse children from what they've seen on the Internet and other forms of pornography. Never before in the history of the earth has such graphic material been available to pervert the minds of young teens. The first wave of their initial offenses will be disastrous to all levels of society; but if they continue to offend after their primary incarcerations, the cost to society will be so overwhelming that we will break under the burden.

Heroes of the Day

The good news is that there are some remarkable people out there working day and night to decrease the size of the wave.

As a further note to the Sandusky story, Matt Sandusky, another of the (adopted) children, revealed (at the time of his father's trial) that his father repeatedly abused him from the time he was just eight until he was 17. The revelation resulted in ostracism by his mother and the rest of the family. Matt now runs a foundation called "Peaceful Hearts" and helps others find their own personal peace. In an interview with Kevin Shelly of the Philly Voice, Matt said, "Nothing should be more important than protecting children... I intend to tell my story until I can't breathe."

After his brother Jeff's arrest, Matt told NBC News that if the allegations are true, "He should not see the outside of a prison cell for the rest of his life. These people need to be stopped. Human beings need to rise up and say, 'Enough is enough.' We need to take a stance and say our priority is protecting children."

Joe Paterno was the head coach for football at Penn State when assistant coach Sandusky was committing his sex crimes against children. Shortly after Sandusky's arrest in 2011, Paterno was fired as the longtime coach of Penn's football team for failing to intervene in the abuse. In his exiting statement, he said, "With the benefit of hindsight, I wish I'd done more."

Joe Paterno's widow, Sue Paterno, along with sons Jay and Scott, took his wish that he had done more as a personal call to action. Since 2012, they have been working with "Stop It Now!" to develop "Circles of Safety for Higher Education," a program to combat child sexual victimization.

With $230,000 in funding from the Paternos, "Stop it Now!" worked with nearly 150 college staff members from across Pennsylvania's 14 state universities, training them in child sexual abuse prevention. [30]

As a further note on the sports page, Dayton Moore, the general manager for the Kansas City Royals, recently spoke up at a press conference about the impact porn can have on players, and the discussions they have as a team on this topic. He said:

"We've done a lot of leadership stuff with our players. Very transparent about things that happen in our game, not only with drugs and alcohol. We talk about pornography, and the effects of what that does to the minds of players and the distractions, and how that leads to abuse of--domestic abuse--to abuse of women. How it impacts

30. Child Sexual Abuse Prevention: Who are the Funders? https://chronicleofsocialchange.org/analysis/child-sexual-abuse-prevention-funders-families-backing Accessed Nov. 07, 2017

relationships--we talk about a lot of things. And I don't mind sharing with you."[31]

Having fingered Internet pornography as one of the most critical factors in the development of a predator, I believe it makes the most sense to dry up the flood of smut. However, draining the Internet of child pornography would seem to be an impossible task. But with modern-day heroes like Jim Gamble, the C.E.O. of the Child Exploitation and Online Protection Centre (CEOP - the United Kingdom's centralized agency for fighting sexual child abuse), there is hope. I first read about him in Julian Sher's book, *One Child at a Time* and, for the first time in a long time, I caught a glimmer of hope that 'the good guys are gonna win.'

The motto of CEOP is, "Making Every Child Matter Everywhere." Launched in the U.K. in 2006 as a centralized clearinghouse run by law enforcement, it fights child abuse with a coalition of specialized disciplines from the computer industry, child protection groups, credit card companies, social agencies, educators and a variety of industries. The different specialties all bring their expertise to the table, providing the widest perspective possible from which to hunt down and catch predators and rescue children from abusive situations. CEOP's international tentacles reach around the world, plucking out people who profit from child trafficking and catching travelers who use child prostitutes in third-world countries.

Jim Gamble has come all the way around the block. He started his work with one goal in mind – catching and arresting offenders. Then his vision widened to save the children who are the subjects of child pornography. Now his focus is on stopping pornographers

---

31. Royals GM Discusses The Dangers Of Porn ... https://deadspin.com/royals-gm-discusses-the-dangers-of-porn-during-danny-du-1798560122 Accessed November 07, 2017

from making the videos or taking the pictures *before* a child is abused.

Working with Jim Gamble in CEOP is Joe Sullivan, a brilliant forensic behavior analyst blessed with an abundance of common sense. Having departed from the wild west philosophy of rounding 'em up and throwing away the key, Joe insists on understanding the offender. He believes that by studying their triggers and their behavior, there is more probability of stopping them. With the numbers of men who admit to fantasizing about having sex with a child, it makes so much more sense to help them deal with their thoughts before they commit a crime than to wait until a child has been victimized and then try to make some sense out of the situation with jails and courts.

Having tried other methods, Jim Gamble recognized Joe Sullivan's wisdom in striving to understand who the predators are and how they think. Julian Sher, in his book, *One Child a Time*, quoted Gamble as saying,

"Let's better understand the nature of the person who commits the crime and then see if we can police this environment in a wholly different way....If we're going to divert people from this, we're not going to do it by continually arrests. We recognize that some offenders are more dangerous than others, but for many of the others we need to have a crime reduction strategy, a diversion strategy.[32]"

Gamble began to take a different tack with his news conferences. He began to appeal to potential predators with less aggression and more reason. He would say, "If you're sitting at home tonight, listening to the radio or watching TV, or reading this article, and you have inappropriate feelings towards children, go and seek help now. Go to your doctor, go to someone you can trust...divert yourself from this

---

32. Sher, Julian (2007). *One Child at a Time*, Random House Canada. p. 60

path. Otherwise, in this day and age, more than likely you're going to destroy your life and that of your family. Because we will catch you.[33]" He firmly believed that the behavior of pedophiles could be influenced and moderated by fear of being caught.

In 2016, another hero of the day, the House of Representatives in the State of Utah publicly declared pornography a 'public health crisis' in the state, prompting the same kind of awareness and education-focused resolution to be passed in numerous other states. It wasn't long before Virginia and South Dakota followed suit.

Expressing concern over rising incidents of crime against children in the fall of 2017 at the People's University in Bhopal, India, Nobel laureate Kailash Satyarthi warned that sexual abuse of children has become a moral epidemic and needs to be tackled on a priority basis. He called on people to join him in his march, a 'Mahayuddha' and raise their voices against the epidemic proportions of child sexual abuse and trafficking. The Bharat Yatra was a 35-day journey from Kanyakumari to Delhi.[34]

Here and there, all around the world, individuals and communities are choosing to take a stand on the right side of history. The voice calling for a future free of pornography, sexual exploitation, and sex trafficking is getting louder. More and more research is being con-ducted that shows the harmful effects of pornography on consumers' brains, relationships, and in society as a whole, clearly categorizing porn as something to be avoided rather than celebrated.

"Fight the New Drug" was formed by a group of young college students who were struck – and shocked – by the science of how porn affects the brain. After further study, they discovered that "porn

33. Ibid.
34. Sexual abuse of children is a moral epidemic: Nobel ...   http://kalamkranti.com/sexual-abuse-children-moral-epidemic-nobel-laureate-kailash-satyarthi/ Accessed November 07, 2017

not only has negative effects on the individual, but that pornography's influence can cause problems in relationships, tearing apart families. Production of pornography is often inseparably connected to the world of sex trafficking and sexual exploitation. The research is clear that pornography has negative neurological effects, is damaging to relationships, and is impacting our society as a whole."[35] They couldn't believe that all of this was happening and nobody was talking about it, so they quickly became passionate about educating the world (specifically youth) and raising awareness on the issue.

In 2009, "Fight the New Drug" officially became a nonprofit organization and began to spread its anti-pornography message across borders of religious beliefs, political agenda, and social backgrounds by presenting it as a public health issue, rather than as a moral, political or religious argument.

As a nonprofit organization, they give live presentations on the harmful effects of pornography in schools (public and private) and universities throughout North America. By 2014, they had toured the country and presented their message to over 300 schools, reaching hundreds of thousands of teens.[36]

Their website, *www.fightthenewdrug.org* has gathered a massive following that has created a powerful social movement online. In addition to spreading awareness, "Fight the New Drug" assists young people who are already struggling with porn addiction through their online program: "The Fortify Program." They not only educate teens on the harmful effects of pornography, but also give them a place to turn for help, as many are silently struggling and are too ashamed or embarrassed to reach out for help.

35. About Fight The New Drug - Fight the New Drug   http://fightthenewdrug.org/about/ Accessed Nov.07, 2017
36. About Fight The New Drug - Fight the New Drug http://fightthenewdrug.org/about/ Accessed November 07, 2017

The Depths of Hell

Award-winning actress, Blake Lively, was an honoree at Variety's 2017 Power of Women dinner. In her speech, she took the opportunity to call attention to the importance of supporting the Child Rescue Coalition, a group that helps identify IP addresses that are trading child pornography, and gives that information to police. The information can be invaluable in the search for the people engaged in the felonious trading of child pornography.[37]

Shining a spotlight on the crisis of child pornography, Lively called for greater awareness and resources to fight the epidemic.

"Sexual exploitation of children is something that isn't happening rarely; it's not happening worlds away," she said. "It's happening right here and right now."

As a mother with two young children, she was devastated upon realizing not only how common child pornography is, but that as viewers of child pornography become desensitized, they start looking for younger and younger children.

She told of a law enforcement officer who has worked in child pornography prevention who told her that he found pornographic videos of infants with their umbilical cords still attached. The acts these children are enduring are unspeakable, she said, including rape, torture, bondage, and bestiality, among other acts.

"Anything you can think of, it's out there, and it's being traded. And it's 30-50 million files a day being traded, that we know of."

Alarmingly, the statistics indicate that the majority of child porn viewers are, or will become, abusers themselves.

---

37. Watch Blake Lively's powerful speech against child ... http://catholicnewsagency.com/news/watch-blake-livelys-powerful-speech-against-child-pornography-77658 Accessed November 07, 2017

The Child Rescue Coalition, in just three years of offering its services free to law enforcement, has helped find 9,000 predators and has saved 2,000 children – and should be supported heavily.

Internet Deterrents

Another hero in the Internet porn war is Detective Sergeant Paul Gillespie, who served the Toronto Police Services for over 27 years. In 2003, Gillespie was running Canada's largest child exploitation unit. Having seized three million pornographic photos of children the previous year,[38] he was overwhelmed with the horrible truth that "the bad guys were winning." It seemed impossible to get on top of the incredibly sophisticated encryption and filtering techniques they were using. It was as if the police would plug one hole in the dike and a leak would spring up in a totally inaccessible location.

Thumb drives, wireless drives, cell phone cameras and portable personal devices are all providing new avenues for the traders and producers of child pornography to send and store their collections. The task of finding a child who is a subject of this material is like searching for a particular grain of sand in a desert.

In frustration, Gillespie hammered off an e-mail to Bill Gates, blaming Microsoft for providing a venue for the explosion of child abuse images on the Internet. He basically said: Your technology helped create this mess; help us clean it up.[39] He never expected a response – but got one.

Gates read the message and contacted Frank Clegg, then the chairman of Microsoft Canada. That led to a meeting of some of the top Microsoft experts with Paul Gillespie and the police. Gillespie

---

38. Sher, Julian (2007). *One Child at a Time,* Random House Canada. p. 64.
39. Ibid, p. 65..

decided that the best way to demonstrate the problem was to show the computer team a handful of the images the police have to deal with every day.

Frank Battison, the senior team leader for the project, described the experience. "He (Gillespie) warns us there are five pictures; turn your heads if you want. It was horrific. Absolutely horrific. I saw one, looked at number two. And I just turned away. Didn't want to see anything else. And to this day I still have those two burned in my head. I want to get rid of them, and I don't know how. But it certainly inspires you to do what you can to eradicate these problems."[40]

When Battison took a look at the archaic resources available to the police for fighting the battle, he was stunned. He said, "The police were being asked to catch pedophiles, and the task would be equivalent to sending somebody out in a rowboat in the middle of an ocean and saying, 'Catch some fish.' And the only fish that they're really able to catch are the ones that jump in the boat!"[41]

The upshot of the meetings between Microsoft and the Toronto police was a decision to cooperate in the building of a database that could compile and connect police data to find links to pedophiles and abused children within the millions of graphics and bits of information. The database was called the Child Exploitation Tracking System (CETS). Microsoft committed to invest several millions of dollars to work towards Paul Gillespie's dream of building CETS into an integrated, international tool available to every law enforcement agency for tracking predators and finding victimized children.

When the police found and rescued the first child through CETS, it was so thrilling that it set Microsoft on the path of investing millions more and enlarging its scope beyond what anyone had hoped was

---

40. Ibid p. 65..
41.Ibid p. 65..

74

possible. Gillespie was encouraged beyond bounds. "We're taking back the Internet. The bad guys have long used it as their communication tool. Well, it's our turn. And we'll see who's left standing."[42]

The reality is that no matter how tirelessly these unsung heroes work, there are always going to be predators who slip through the cracks and molest our children. That's why we can't lay down our vigilance.

Getting Help

For those addicted to pornography who sincerely want help, the idea of having people find out can be prohibitive. Many addicts are high profile, upstanding citizens of the community with a lot to lose. The probability of rejection and ostracism is very real and too great to risk. While it would be wonderful to think that a request for help would be met with understanding and willingness to assist in healing, recovery, and restoration, the reality is that it's difficult to find effective treatment in the community. Thankfully, help is available from the same source pornography addicts feed their addictions – the Internet. In the same way they hide their dark activities, they can, if they so desire, be anonymous in the process of restoration.

The problem is that porn thrives on shame and secrets. The key to the solution lies in eliminating the shame and secrecy without falling prey to the loose tongues of gossips and other untrustworthy groups or individuals.

The allure of pornography is governed by three main factors: accessibility, affordability, and anonymity.[43] Like a three-legged stool, when the leg of anonymity is broken, the allure of pornography collapses.

---

42. Sher, Julian (2007). *One Child at a Time*, Random House Canada p. 68.
43. The late psychologist, Dr. Al Cooper, Cooper, Cybersex: The Dark Side of the Force (London: Brunner-Routledge, 2000).

Internet accountability services are designed to help those struggling with porn to overcome their addiction by monitoring their Internet activity and sending a report to a designated, trustworthy[44] friend who holds them accountable for their online choices, breaking anonymity in safety. The information in the report can be used in an honest discussion with this trusted individual to help the addict break free. It's all about the power of transparency and relationships.

When someone trying to break free from addiction knows that someone they trust will receive a report of the websites they visit, it changes how they use the web. It not only breaks the anonymity but also reduces the *temptation* to click on inappropriate links.

Covenant Eyes (www.covenanteyes.com) is one such service I can recommend for its excellence and user-friendly accessibility. It's not expensive and can be installed on all one's devices. It monitors and keeps a record of Internet browsing for the designated accountability partner. Besides monitoring, it provides an option for totally blocking the bad stuff – a great help for parents dealing with numerous computers.

The following are more suggested links to freedom:
HTTP: / / x3watch.com /
HTTP: / / www.no-porn.com / breaking.html

And then there's the "Conquer Series" of videos.
HTTPS://conquerseries.com

Filmmaking couple, Jeremy and Tiana Wiles and their team at KingdomWorks Studios produced a small group seminar for men, featuring ten interactive seminars by former U.S. Marine fighter pilot, Dr. Ted Roberts. Thirty years of his knowledge and experience has been condensed into six hours of study. The Series includes

44. Remember that there's a difference between "trusted" and "trustworthy."

cinematic reenactments and compelling interviews with contemporary role models. While it is unabashedly faith-based, anyone, whether faith-oriented or agnostic, will find it to be a comprehensive approach that offers genuine help for a way out of addiction to porn.

I know of no other cinematic teaching series to help men get to the root of their addiction to pornography while offering proven principles and practical tools to conquer its hold on their lives. Unrivaled in its scope, the series has been used by over 450,000 men in more than 65 countries with a 90 percent success rate! While it was designed for use in small groups, it is also ideal for self-study. Worn-out behavior modification techniques have been replaced by functional strategies to achieve actual change of core desires and responses.

If my ex-husband had had the opportunity to access this material, life might have been a lot different for our family.

Testimonials abound to the effectiveness of the series. Here's one: "I absolutely love this disc series!!! This is how good it is: our 19 and 17-year-old sons exist in their phones – texting, listening to music. When my husband and I were watching the DVDs, we saw them looking at (the television) and occasionally look at their phone. Not 15 minutes in, we saw them put down their phones, take the earbuds out of their ears and watch intensely. Each time we put in the DVDs, the phones went down, and they watched and took in all that was being said. Currently, my husband is using this series at the University he works at." – Tammy Miller from Canton, Ohio.

I have nothing to gain from suggesting any of these resources, other than the hope that people will take advantage of what they have to offer and spare themselves and their families the devastation experienced by my family.

Accepting Responsibility

The message of raw pornography is regurgitated by the general media's negative depiction of women and the rendering of sexual relationships to the base usage of flesh. Until the message of the media is changed, legislation is going to have little effect on how people view physical bodies.

To protect the most vulnerable members of society, we have to move away from viewing sexuality as a commodity and re-render it to its place in healthy relationships. That involves the necessity of the media working to protect the innocence of childhood and finding more creative ways to sell products than through billboard-sized pictures of body parts. Titillation and disregard for the value of women and children have no place in the entertainment industry or the marketing of goods and services.

When children are inundated with images of sex and violence day after day on television, in comics and video games, the messages of pornography become more reasonable and acceptable to them. They become *pornographied*.

The media must begin to monitor itself. It has made aggression edgy and chic. When translated from the brain of a viewer into real-life, there can be dreadful repercussions – and there's no scroll of the cast of characters at the end.

Healing society starts with us individually in our own homes, teaching our children to love and be loved, teaching them wholesome values so that they will make healthy choices. Taking time to communicate empathy, consideration, and selfless love to the little ones we bring into the world is the turning point for healing our world.

My Task

In doing the research for this booklet, I've touched down in the depths of hell. Even though I've taken the journey as a tourist rather than a citizen, I have had no stomach for painting travelogue pictures. I have had no desire to take you there. To make my points, I've had to be more explicit than I'd like to have been.

My task has not been to expose every facet of modern pornography. It has been to show that it is linked to crimes against children and vulnerable people of all ages. I am one small voice begging sane people not to indulge in it before they lose their humanity, their ability to have healthy relationships and risk turning their fantasies into criminal behavior which could not only land them in jail but leave a trail of destroyed victims.

My task has been to shake naive parents who may be trapped in the philosophy of a pornographied culture and say, "You have been given the privilege of shaping a life. Keep your mind strong and healthy so that you can raise healthy kids. Don't warp your child by allowing pornography anywhere near your home where he or she could come upon it. Recognize its incredible toxicity in the life of your family."

My message is that pornography is not just junk food for perverts – it's the main diet for people who molest our children. I'd like to see it wiped off the face of this planet.

My life is an example of how an addiction to pornography can shatter the lives of everyone whose lives can touch that of the addict. Had my ex-husband not become hooked while on a summer visit as a teen with a relative, our whole family would have celebrated Thanksgiving together this year – as we always did. It was always my favorite time of year. I loved going out in the woods, cutting gloriously colored branches to decorate our home while the aroma of stuffed turkey gave promise to the meal we would soon enjoy together. I loved the happy giggles of grandchildren and aunts and uncles delighting in the precious bonds of family. I loved sitting around the dining table together, feasting on the smiles of precious faces. Together. And now it's gone. The precious ones have scattered all across the continent, shell-shocked by the betrayal of the husband I never really knew.

My call-to-action is for you to join your voice with the modern-day heroes mentionned and to others who are fighting the pornographication of society. We can make a huge change in this world by doing everything possible in our own corners of the world to eliminate pornography. I'm not naîve. I know there will always be pornography. But maybe our efforts will stop one teenage boy or girl from viewing it, who would otherwise have eventually molested one child. The whole world, for that one protected child, would be a different world.

For Further Reading...

Abel, G., Becker, J., Mittleman, M., Rouleau, J., and Murphy, W. (1987). Journal of Interpersonal Violence, 2(1), March

Beauregard, M and O'Leary, D. (2007). *The Spiritual Brain*, A Neuroscientist's Case for the Existence of the Soul, HarperOne, San Francisco, CA

The Holy Bible, The New International Version, Zondervan Bible Publishers, Grand Rapids, Michigan.

Birchall, E. (1989). The Frequency of Child Abuse – What do We Really Know?, in Colton, Matthew and Vanstone, Maurice (1996). *Betrayal of Trust*; Sexual Abuse by Men Who Work With Children, , London ON: Free Association Books Ltd.

Bremner, Dr. J. Douglas (2007). The Lasting Effects of Psychological Trauma on Memory and the Hippocampus, Law and Psychiatry,

Briggs, F., & Hawkins, R.M.F. (1996). A comparison of the childhood experiences of convicted male child molesters and men who were sexually abused in childhood and claimed to be non offenders. Child Abuse and Neglect

Browne, A., & Finkelhor, D. (1986). Initial and long-term effects: A review of the research. In D. Finkelhor, A Sourcebook on Child Sexual Abuse, Beverly Hills: Sage

Bushman, B.J., Baumeister, R.F., & Stack, A.D. (1999). Catharsis, aggression and persuasive influence: Self-fulfilling or self-defeating prophecies? Journal of Personality and Social Psychology

Butler, Sandra (1985). *Conspiracy of Silence: The Trauma of Incest,* San Francisco, Volcano Press.

Carnes, Patrick (1994). *Out of the Shadows*; Understanding Sexual Addiction, Center City, Minnesota: Hazelden Foundation

Carter, Wm. Lee (2002). *A Teen's Guide to Overcoming Sexual Abuse;* It Happened to Me, Oakland, Ca., New Harbinger Publications, Inc.

Colton, Matthew and Vanstone, Maurice (1996). *Betrayal of Trust*; Sexual Abuse by Men Who Work With Children, , London ON: Free Association Books Ltd.

Diagnostic and Statistical Manual of Mental Disorders (DSM 111-R), The American Psychological Association, 1987

Elliott, M., Browne, K., & Kilcoyne, J. (1995). *Child Sexual Abuse Prevention: What Offenders Tell Us*, Child Abuse & Neglect

Fink, Paul (2005). *Science,* Vol. 309, August.

Finkelhor, D. (1984). *Child Sexual Abuse: New Theory and Research*, New York: Free Press

Finkelhor, D. and associates (eds) (1986), *A Sourcebook on Child Sexual Abuse*, Newbury Park, CA.: Sage

Finkelhor, D., Hotaling, G., Lewis, I. and Smith, C. (1990) Sexual Abuse in a National Survey of Adult Men and Women; Prevalence Characteristics and Risk Factors, *Child Abuse and Neglect*

Finkelhor, D. (1994). The International epidemiology of child sexual abuse. Child Abuse & Neglect, 18

Finkelhor, D. and Dziuba-Leatherman, J. (1995). Victimization prevention programs: A national survey of children's exposure and reactions, Child Abuse & Neglect

Finney, Lynne D. (1992). *Reach for the Rainbow*; Advance Healing for Survivors of Sexual Abuse, New York: The Putnam Publishing Group

Forward, Susan, and Craig Buck (1979). *Betrayal of Innocence: Incest and its Devastation,* New York: Penguin Books

Genesee Justice Family (2005). *Genesee Justice 2005*; Instruments of Law, Order and Peace, Batavia, N.Y., Genesee Justice Family Research & Development

Groth, N., Burgess, A., Birnbaum, H. and Gary, T. (1978). A study of the child molester. Myths and realities. *LAE Journal of the American Criminal Justice Association*, 41(1), Winter/Spring.

Halliday, L. (1985). *Sexual Abuse:* Counseling issues and concerns. Campbell River, B.C., Ptarmigan Press

Hergenhahn, B.R. (1992). *An Introduction to the History of Psychology.* Belmont, CA: Wadsworth Publishing Company.

Hopper, Dr. J. (2007). Child Abuse: Statistics, Research and Resources Jacob Wetterling Foundation website's frequently asked questions section

Knopp, Fay Honey (1982). *Remedial Intervention in Adolescent Sex Offenses*; Nine Program Descriptions, Brooklyn, N.Y.: Faculty Press, Inc.

Leaf , Dr. Caroline (2007). *Who Switched Off My Brain?*, Switch on Your Brain, Rivonia, South Africa

Lilienfeld, Scott O. and Lambert, Kelly (Oct. 2007). Brain Stains, Scientific American

MacAulay, The Honourable Lawrence - Solicitor General Canada (2001). *High-Risk Offenders;* A Handbook for Criminal Justice Professionals, The Gov't of Canada

Marshall, Dr. W.L. and Barrett, Sylvia (1990). *Criminal Neglect*; Why Sex Offenders Go Free, Toronto: Doubleday Canada Limited

Matthews, Dr. Frederick (1995). *Breaking Silence - Creating Hope*; Help for Adults Who Molest Children, Ottawa: National Clearinghouse on Family Violence, Health Canada

McCoy, D. (2006). *The Manipulative Man*, Adams Media, Avon, Mass

Mercy, J. A. (1999). Having New Eyes: Viewing Child Sexual Abuse as a Public Health Problem. Sexual Abuse: A Journal of Research and Treatment

Michel, Lou and Herbeck, Dan, *Confessions of a Child Porn Addict,* The Buffalo News, Oct. 21, 2007

Minnery, Tom (1986). *Pornography; A Human Tragedy*, Wheaton, Illinois, Tyndale House Publishers Inc., Dr. J. Dobson

Murr, Doris C. (2004). *Dorie's Secret*, Kitchener, Ontario, Pandora Press

Peck, M. Scott (1983). *People of the Lie*, New York, Touchstone - Simon & Schuster Inc.

Posten, Carol and Lison, Karen (1990). *Reclaiming our Lives*; Hope for Adult Survivors of Incest, Boston, MA: Little, Brown & Company

Pryor, Douglas W. (1996). *Unspeakable Acts*; Why Men Sexually Abuse Children, New York and London: New York University Press

Public Health Agency of Canada (2007), National Clearinghouse on Family Violence.

Reavill, Gil (2005). *Smut;* A Sex Industry Insider (and Concerned father) says Enough is Enough, London, England, Penguin Books, Ltd.

Rush, F. (1980). *The Best Kept Secret:* Sexual abuse of children. New York, McGraw-Hill Book Company

The San Francisco Chronicle (April 3, 2005)

Salter, Anna C. (1988). *Treating Child Sex Offenders and Victims*; A Practical Guide, Newbury Park, California: SAGE Publications, Inc.

Salter, Anna C. (2003). *Predators: Pedophiles, Rapists and Other Sex Offenders*, New York: Basic Books

Science Daily, July 30, 2007. News release issued by Stanford University Medical Centre

Seligman, M.E.P. (1994). *What You Can Change and What You Can't,* New York: Alfred A. Knopf.

Sher, Julian (2007). *One Child at a Time,* Random House Canada

Singer, P. (1991). Ethics. *The New Encyclopedia Britannica*, Volume 18, Edition 15

UN Secretary General's Study on Violence Against Children (2006) Section II.B

Van Dam, Carla (2001). *Identifying Child Molesters;* Preventing Child Sexual Abuse by Recognizing the Patterns of the Offenders, New York: The Halworth Maltreatment and Trauma Press

Wholey, Sam (1992). *When the Worst That Can Happen Already Has*; Conquering Life's Most Difficult Times, New York: Hyperion

Yantzi, Mark (1998). *Sexual Offending and Restoration*, Waterloo, Ontario and Scottdale, Pa., Herald Press

About Diane Roblin-Lee (Sharp)

Diane Roblin-Lee, award-winning author, former social-worker, and e ducator, has (out of personal heartbreak) done extensive research in the field of child sexual abuse and the role played by pornography.

She has written over twenty books on a variety of subjects, Diane's passion has always been for the family – not only her own, but also in recognition of its importance as the basic unit of society. With the theme of family running through all of her work, Diane has been politically active, hosted several TV programs (including NiteLite for seven years) and served for many years on the board of the Heart to Heart Marriage and Family Institute.

Her legacy journal, *To My Family...My Life Legacy,* is a priceless resource for those wishing to bless their families with the insights, wisdom and experience gained through their lifetimes.

Remarried in 2013, Diane and her second husband, Morgan Sharp, are committed to helping to ensure the protection of children everywhere, through whatever means possible.

For further information on

Training Workshops and Speakers
Information and Training Materials, please contact:

Plan to Protect ®
117 Ringwood Dr., Unit #11
Stouffville, ON CAN L4A 8C1
www.plantoprotect.com 1-877-455-3555

*Other Books by Diane
can be seen at*

www.bydesignmedia.ca

Lightning Source UK Ltd.
Milton Keynes UK
UKHW020715130622
404345UK00010B/968

9 781896 213521